Lipton

CREATIVE COOKERY

MADE EASY WITH LIPTON SOUP MIX

PUBLICATIONS INTERNATIONAL, LTD.

CONTENTS

MICROWAVE DIRECTIONS
Microwave ovens vary in wattage and power output; therefore, the microwave cooking times given may need to be adjusted according to your oven.

© 1987 Thomas J. Lipton, Inc.

Lipton is a registered trademark of Thomas J. Lipton, Inc. Englewood Cliffs, New Jersey 07632.

Project Director/Editor: Anna Marie Coccia, Manager — Test Kitchens
Recipe Development and Food Styling: Alyssa A. Alia
Kitchen Associate: Wendy Walters
Publicist: Janet Thompson
Photographer: Daniel J. Piszczatoski
Photography Director: Kevin McCoy, Paino Promotions
Prop Stylist: Stacey Smith

Publications International, Ltd.
7373 N. Cicero Avenue
Lincolnwood
Illinois 60646

Library of Congress Catalog Card Number: 87-60615

ISBN: 0-88176-911-8

Pictured on front cover, clockwise from top right: Pork Steaks with Peppers *(see page 48)*, Thick 'n Cheesy Vegetable Pizza *(see page 88)*, Chicken Breasts Florentine *(see page 44)*, Cool and Creamy Cucumber Spread *(see page 9)*.

Pictured on back cover, clockwise from top right: Fettuccine with Shrimp and Creamy Herb Sauce *(see page 54)*, Wisconsin Cheese 'n Beer Soup *(see page 31)*, Homestyle Zucchini & Tomatoes *(see page 32)*, Quick 'n Easy Tacos and Quick Corn Bread with Chilies 'n Cheese *(see page 78)*.

CARVAJAL S.A.
Impreso en Colombia
Printed in Colombia

The trend in contemporary cooking is toward recipes that are creative, quick and convenient but also designed for today's more discriminating palates. That's what this cookbook is all about!

Whether you're looking for a party-stopping appetizer, a quick family meal, hearty soup recipes or impressive entertaining ideas, you'll find it in this collection...along with much more. We've also included many microwave directions and a section on Stop 'n Go Foods, our answer for today's busy lifestyles.

The beauty of many of these recipes is that they use household ingredients commonly found in your kitchen, ideal for last-minute menu preparation. For those very special meal occasions, the Formal Affairs section features elegant ingredients that require a little more effort but with deliciously satisfying results.

The key to these recipes is the winning combination of ingredients seasoned with Lipton Soup Mix. Each envelope of soup mix contains the perfect blend of seasonings and vegetable pieces that adds convenience to any meal occasion. And, they contain no artificial ingredients or preservatives.

Spark up your meals with these quick, creative and contemporary recipe ideas. We're sure you'll love the results!

Quick 'n Easy Tacos   Quick Corn Bread with Chilies 'n Cheese

SNACKS & STARTERS

DIP IN

❖ WARM MUSHROOM & BACON DIP

6 slices bacon
1/2 pound mushrooms, thinly sliced
2 medium cloves garlic, finely chopped
1 envelope Lipton Golden Onion or Onion Recipe
    Soup Mix
1/8 teaspoon pepper
1 package (8 ounces) cream cheese, softened
1/2 pint (8 ounces) sour cream
    Assorted sliced breads or crackers

In medium skillet, cook bacon; remove and crumble.
Reserve 2 1/2 tablespoons drippings. Add mushrooms
and garlic to reserved drippings and cook over
medium heat, stirring occasionally, 5 minutes or until
mushrooms are tender and liquid is almost evaporated.
Add golden onion recipe soup mix and pepper, then
cream cheese; combine thoroughly. Simmer, stirring
constantly, until cream cheese is melted. Stir in sour
cream and bacon; heat through. Garnish, if desired,
with parsley and additional mushrooms and bacon.
Serve with breads.   *Makes about 2 cups dip*

MICROWAVE DIRECTIONS: In 2-quart casserole,
arrange bacon; loosely cover with paper towel. Heat at
HIGH (Full Power) 6 minutes or until done, turning
casserole once; remove bacon and crumble. Reserve
2 1/2 tablespoons drippings. Add mushrooms and garlic
to reserved drippings and heat uncovered 2 minutes or
until mushrooms are tender, stirring once. Add golden
onion recipe soup mix and pepper, then cream cheese;
combine thoroughly. Decrease heat to MEDIUM (50%
Full Power) and heat uncovered, stirring frequently, 3
minutes or until cream cheese is melted. Stir in sour
cream and bacon. Heat uncovered at MEDIUM
3 minutes or until heated through, stirring once.
Garnish and serve as above.

❖ HOT ARTICHOKE DIP

1 package (9 ounces) frozen artichoke hearts,
    thawed
1/2 pint (8 ounces) sour cream
1/4 cup grated Parmesan cheese
1 envelope Lipton Golden Onion Recipe Soup Mix
    Buttered bread crumbs
    Suggested Dippers*

Preheat oven to 350°.

In food processor or blender, puree artichokes. Add
sour cream and cheese; process until smooth. Stir in
golden onion recipe soup mix. Turn into 2 1/2-cup
casserole, then top with bread crumbs. Bake uncovered
30 minutes or until heated through. Serve with
Suggested Dippers.   *Makes about 2 1/4 cups dip*

*Suggested Dippers: Use carrot or celery sticks, whole
mushrooms or sliced zucchini.

MICROWAVE DIRECTIONS: Omit bread crumbs.
Prepare mixture as above. Heat at HIGH (Full Power),
turning casserole occasionally, 8 minutes or until
heated through. Let stand covered 5 minutes. Serve as
above.

❖ CREAMY HERB DIP

In small bowl, thoroughly blend 1 envelope Lipton
Creamy Herb Recipe Soup Mix with 1 pint (16 ounces)
sour cream. Chill at least 2 hours. Serve with assorted
fresh vegetables or chips.   *Makes about 2 cups dip*

Warm Mushroom & Bacon Dip

ROASTED RED PEPPER DIP

1 envelope Lipton Onion or Onion-Mushroom
   Recipe Soup Mix
1/2 pint (8 ounces) sour cream
1 jar (7 ounces) roasted red peppers packed in oil,
   undrained
1/2 teaspoon basil leaves
1/4 teaspoon oregano
   Suggested Dippers*

In food processor or blender, combine all ingredients
except Suggested Dippers until smooth. Chill at least 2
hours. Serve with Suggested Dippers.

Makes about 2 cups dip

*Suggested Dippers: Use mozzarella sticks, bread
sticks, sliced pepperoni, cooked tortellini, pitted ripe
olives or cherry tomatoes.

FRESH HERB DIP

1 cup loosely packed fresh basil leaves
1/2 cup slivered almonds
1/4 cup loosely packed fresh parsley
1/4 cup olive or vegetable oil
1 small clove garlic, chopped
1/2 pint (8 ounces) sour cream
1/4 cup grated Parmesan cheese
1 envelope Lipton Golden Onion Recipe Soup Mix
   Suggested Dippers*

In food processor or blender, combine basil, almonds,
parsley, oil and garlic until smooth. Add sour cream,
cheese and golden onion recipe soup mix; process
until smooth. Chill at least 2 hours. Serve with
Suggested Dippers.   *Makes about 2 cups dip*

*Suggested Dippers: Use mozzarella sticks, bread sticks,
cooked spinach or egg tortellini, or cherry tomatoes.

From top to bottom: Double Bean Dip, Fresh Herb Dip, Roasted Red Pepper Dip

❖ DOUBLE BEAN DIP

1 envelope Lipton Golden Onion Recipe Soup Mix
1 can (16 ounces) chick peas or garbanzos, rinsed and drained
1 can (16 ounces) white kidney or cannellini beans, rinsed and drained
1/4 cup olive or vegetable oil
1 tablespoon finely chopped parsley
2 teaspoons lemon juice
1 small clove garlic, chopped
1/4 teaspoon pepper
    Suggested Dippers*

In food processor or mixing bowl, combine all ingredients except Suggested Dippers until almost smooth. Chill at least 2 hours. Serve with Suggested Dippers.   *Makes about 3 cups dip*

*Suggested Dippers: Use pita bread cut into triangles, bread sticks, snow peas, carrot sticks or assorted crackers.

❖ NACHO CHEESE DIP

In small bowl, thoroughly blend 1 envelope Lipton Nacho Cheese Recipe Soup Mix with 1 pint (16 ounces) sour cream. Chill at least 2 hours. Serve with tortilla, corn or potato chips.   *Makes about 2 cups dip*

❖ BAKED CLAM DIP

1 envelope Lipton Vegetable Recipe Soup Mix
2 packages (8 ounces each) cream cheese, softened
2 cans (61/2 ounces each) minced or chopped clams, drained (reserve 1/2 cup liquid)
1/2 teaspoon oregano
1/8 teaspoon pepper
6 slices bacon, crisp-cooked and crumbled*
    Buttered bread crumbs
    Suggested Dippers**

Preheat oven to 350°.

In food processor or blender, combine vegetable recipe soup mix, cream cheese, clams, reserved liquid, oregano and pepper; process until smooth. Stir in bacon. Turn into lightly greased 1-quart casserole, then top with bread crumbs. Bake uncovered 20 minutes or until heated through. Serve with Suggested Dippers.
                                    Makes about 3 cups dip

*Substitution: Use 1 tablespoon bacon bits.

**Suggested Dippers: Use assorted crackers, fresh vegetables or sliced breads.

MICROWAVE DIRECTIONS: Prepare mixture as above. Heat uncovered at HIGH (Full Power) 4 minutes or until heated through. Let stand covered 2 minutes. Serve as above.

❖ LIPTON CALIFORNIA DIP

In small bowl, blend 1 envelope Lipton Onion Recipe Soup Mix with 1 pint (16 ounces) sour cream; chill.
                                    Makes about 2 cups dip

For a creamier dip, add more sour cream.

Try these delicious variations!
● **CALIFORNIA SEAFOOD DIP:** Add 1 cup finely chopped cooked clams, crabmeat or shrimp, 1/4 cup chili sauce and 1 tablespoon horseradish.

● **CALIFORNIA BACON DIP:** Add 1/3 cup crumbled cooked bacon or bacon bits.

● **CALIFORNIA BLUE CHEESE DIP:** Add 1/4 pound crumbled blue cheese and 1/4 cup finely chopped walnuts.

PARTY TIP

For an attractive presentation, serve this popular Lipton favorite in a hollowed head of iceberg lettuce or cabbage. Arrange on a wicker tray or in a straw basket, then surround with an assortment of brightly colored fresh vegetables such as broccoli, carrots, cauliflower, celery, mushrooms, bell peppers and radishes.

❖ CHILI CON QUESO

2 tablespoons butter or margarine
1 envelope Lipton Onion Recipe Soup Mix
3 tablespoons all-purpose flour
1 cup (1/2 pint) light cream or half and half
1 can (141/2 ounces) whole peeled tomatoes, undrained and chopped
1 can (4 ounces) chopped green chilies, drained
2 cups shredded Monterey Jack or Muenster cheese (about 6 ounces)
    Tortilla chips or bread cubes

In medium saucepan, melt butter over medium heat and blend in onion recipe soup mix, flour and cream. Bring just to the boiling point, stirring frequently, then simmer, stirring occasionally, until sauce is thickened, about 5 minutes. Add tomatoes, chilies and cheese. Simmer, stirring constantly, until cheese is melted. Turn into fondue pot or chafing dish and serve warm with tortilla chips.   *Makes about 2 cups fondue*

MICROWAVE DIRECTIONS: In 11/2-quart casserole, heat butter at HIGH (Full Power) 1 minute. Blend in onion recipe soup mix, flour and cream. Heat uncovered, stirring occasionally, 2 minutes or until sauce is thickened. Stir in tomatoes and chilies and heat uncovered 5 minutes, stirring once. Stir in cheese and heat 1 minute or until cheese is melted. Serve as above.

❖ GUACAMOLE DIP

1 cup Lipton California Dip (see page 7)
2 medium avocados, coarsely chopped (about 2 cups)
1 can (4 ounces) chopped green chilies, drained
2 teaspoons lemon juice
1/4 teaspoon hot pepper sauce
Suggested Dippers*

In medium bowl, combine all ingredients except Suggested Dippers; chill. Serve with Suggested Dippers.
Makes about 2 1/2 cups dip

*Suggested Dippers: Use tortilla, corn or potato chips, sliced green or red pepper, or tomato wedges.

❖ HOT 'N CREAMY VEGETABLE DIP

1 envelope Lipton Vegetable Recipe Soup Mix
1 container (15 ounces) ricotta cheese
3/4 cup shredded Monterey Jack cheese (about 2 1/2 ounces)
6 slices bacon, crisp-cooked and crumbled
Assorted crackers

Preheat oven to 350°.

In 1-quart casserole, combine vegetable recipe soup mix, ricotta, 1/2 cup Monterey Jack cheese and bacon. Top with remaining Monterey Jack cheese and bake uncovered 30 minutes or until heated through. Serve with crackers. *Makes about 2 1/2 cups dip*

MICROWAVE DIRECTIONS: In 1-quart casserole, combine vegetable recipe soup mix, ricotta, 1/2 cup Monterey Jack cheese and bacon. Heat uncovered at HIGH (Full Power) 6 minutes, stirring every 2 minutes. Top with remaining Monterey Jack cheese and heat an additional 2 minutes. Let stand covered 5 minutes. Serve as above.

❖ ZESTY MUSTARD DIP

1 envelope Lipton Golden Onion Recipe Soup Mix
1/2 pint (8 ounces) sour cream
1/2 pint (8 ounces) plain yogurt
1/4 cup yellow, Dijon-style or brown prepared mustard
1/8 teaspoon pepper
Suggested Dippers*

In small bowl, thoroughly blend all ingredients except Suggested Dippers; chill. Serve with Suggested Dippers. *Makes about 2 cups dip*

*Suggested Dippers: Use bread sticks, Muenster cheese sticks, assorted fresh vegetables or crackers.

❖ MEDITERRANEAN TONNATO DIP

1 envelope Lipton Golden Onion Recipe Soup Mix
1 pint (16 ounces) sour cream
1 can (6 1/2 ounces) tuna, drained and flaked
1/4 cup coarsely chopped oil-cured (Mediterranean-style) black olives*
1 tablespoon capers, rinsed and drained (optional)
1 tablespoon lemon juice
Suggested Dippers**

In small bowl, thoroughly blend all ingredients except Suggested Dippers; chill. Serve with Suggested Dippers. *Makes about 3 cups dip*

*Substitution: Use 1/4 cup coarsely chopped pitted ripe olives and add 1 tablespoon olive oil.

**Suggested Dippers: Use assorted crackers or fresh vegetables, bread sticks or pepperoni slices.

❖ EXTRA SPECIAL SPINACH DIP

In medium bowl, blend 1 envelope Lipton Vegetable Recipe Soup Mix, 1 pint (16 ounces) sour cream, 1/2 cup mayonnaise and 1/2 teaspoon lemon juice. Stir in 1 package (10 ounces) frozen chopped spinach, thawed and squeezed dry, and 1 can (8 ounces) water chestnuts, drained and chopped; chill.
Makes about 3 cups dip

Try these tempting variations: Stir in 2 tablespoons chopped green onion, radishes or crumbled blue cheese; or omit water chestnuts and add 1 cup chopped apple.

❖ LIPTON VEGETABLE DIP

In small bowl, blend 1 envelope Lipton Vegetable Recipe Soup Mix with 1 pint (16 ounces) sour cream. Chill at least 2 hours. Serve with assorted fresh vegetables or chips. *Makes about 2 cups dip*

For a heartier dip, use 2 envelopes Lipton Vegetable Recipe Soup Mix.

Try these delicious variations!
● **SENSATIONAL SPINACH DIP:** Add 1 package (10 ounces) frozen chopped spinach, thawed and squeezed dry.

● **VEGETABLE CHEESE DIP:** Add 1/4 cup grated Parmesan cheese.

● **CALICO SEAFOOD DIP:** Add 1 cup finely chopped cooked shrimp or crabmeat.

● **GINGER 'N NUT:** Add 1/3 cup chopped peanuts and 1/2 teaspoon ground ginger.

❖ COOL AND CREAMY CUCUMBER SPREAD

3 medium cucumbers
1 (8-ounce) *plus* 1 (3-ounce) package cream
    cheese, softened
1/2 cup sour cream
1/4 cup snipped fresh dill*
1 1/2 teaspoons lemon juice
1 envelope Lipton Vegetable Recipe Soup Mix

Thinly slice 1 cucumber and arrange in bottom of lightly oiled 4-cup ring mold; set aside.

Peel, seed and coarsely chop remaining cucumbers. With food processor or electric mixer, combine cream cheese, 1 cup chopped cucumber, sour cream, dill, lemon juice and vegetable recipe soup mix until smooth. Stir in remaining chopped cucumber. Turn into prepared mold; chill until firm, at least 3 hours. To serve, unmold onto serving platter and fill center, if desired, with cherry tomatoes and leaf lettuce. Serve with assorted crackers.

Makes about 3 1/2 cups spread

*Substitution: Use 2 tablespoons dried dill weed.

❖ FOUR CHEESE SPREAD

1 package (8 ounces) cream cheese, softened
1 cup shredded Swiss cheese (about 4 ounces)
1 cup shredded fontina or Monterey Jack cheese
    (about 3 ounces)
1/2 cup sour cream
1/4 cup grated Parmesan cheese
1/4 cup finely chopped fresh basil leaves*
1 tablespoon finely chopped parsley
1 tablespoon lemon juice
1 envelope Lipton Vegetable Recipe Soup Mix

Line 4-cup mold or bowl with wax paper or dampened cheesecloth; set aside.

With food processor or electric mixer, combine all ingredients until smooth. Pack into prepared mold; cover and chill 2 hours or until firm. To serve, unmold onto serving platter, then remove wax paper. Garnish, if desired, with additional chopped parsley and basil. Serve with assorted crackers, bagel chips or cucumber slices.   *Makes about 3 1/2 cups spread*

*Substitution: Use 1 1/2 teaspoons dried basil leaves.

Cool and Creamy Cucumber Spread

FINGER FOODS

❖ PUFF PASTRY CHEESE TWISTS

1 envelope Lipton Golden Onion Recipe Soup Mix
1/4 cup grated Parmesan cheese
2 teaspoons chili powder
1 teaspoon ground cumin
1 package (17 1/4 ounces) frozen puff pastry
    sheets, thawed

Preheat oven to 425°.

In medium bowl, combine all ingredients except pastry sheets; set aside.

Unfold 1 pastry sheet and sprinkle with 1/2 soup mixture; top with remaining pastry sheet. With rolling pin, lightly roll layered sheets into a 15 × 11-inch rectangle. Sprinkle top pastry sheet with remaining soup mixture, then, with rolling pin, lightly roll mixture into pastry. Cut pastry into 30 (1/2 × 11-inch) strips; twist strips. Arrange on two ungreased baking sheets. Decrease heat to 350° and bake 12 minutes or until golden brown. *Makes about 30 twists*

❖ MINI MONTE CRISTO SANDWICHES

2 tablespoons butter or margarine, softened
2 tablespoons prepared mustard
8 slices white bread
4 slices fontina or Swiss cheese (about 4 ounces)
4 slices cooked ham (about 4 ounces)
3 eggs
1/2 cup milk
1 envelope Lipton Golden Onion Recipe Soup Mix
1/4 cup butter or margarine

Blend 2 tablespoons butter with mustard; evenly spread on each bread slice. Equally top 4 bread slices with cheese and ham; top with remaining bread, buttered side down. Cut each sandwich into 4 triangles.

Beat eggs, milk and golden onion recipe soup mix until well blended. Dip sandwiches in egg mixture, coating well.

In large skillet, melt 1/4 cup butter and cook sandwiches over medium heat, turning once, until golden.
Makes about 16 mini sandwiches

❖ CAJUN-STYLE CHICKEN NUGGETS

1 envelope Lipton Onion or Onion-Mushroom
    Recipe Soup Mix
1/2 cup plain dry bread crumbs
1 1/2 teaspoons chili powder
1 teaspoon ground cumin
1 teaspoon thyme leaves
1/4 teaspoon red pepper
2 pounds boneless chicken breasts, cut into 1-inch
    pieces
Oil

In large bowl, combine onion recipe soup mix, bread crumbs, chili powder, cumin, thyme and pepper. Dip chicken in bread crumb mixture, coating well.

In large skillet, heat 1/2 inch oil and cook chicken over medium heat, turning once, until done; drain on paper towels. Serve warm and, if desired, with assorted mustards. *Makes about 5 dozen nuggets*

MICROWAVE DIRECTIONS: Prepare chicken as above. In 13 × 9-inch baking dish, arrange chicken, then drizzle with 2 to 3 tablespoons oil. Heat uncovered at HIGH (Full Power) 6 minutes or until chicken is done, rearranging chicken once; drain on paper towels. Serve as above.

❖ MINI COCKTAIL MEATBALLS

1 envelope Lipton Onion, Onion-Mushroom, Beefy
    Mushroom or Beefy Onion Recipe Soup Mix
1 pound ground beef
1/2 cup plain dry bread crumbs
1/4 cup dry red wine or water
2 eggs, slightly beaten

Preheat oven to 375°.

In medium bowl, combine all ingredients; shape into 1-inch meatballs.

In shallow baking pan, arrange meatballs and bake 18 minutes or until done. Serve, if desired, with assorted mustards or tomato sauce.

Makes about 4 dozen meatballs

Puff Pastry Cheese Twists
Cajun-Style Chicken Nuggets

❖ SPINACH RICE BALLS

1½ cups cooked rice
1 package (10 ounces) frozen chopped spinach,
    cooked and well drained
½ cup shredded mozzarella cheese (about 1½
    ounces)
⅓ cup plain dry bread crumbs
2 eggs, slightly beaten
¼ cup grated Parmesan cheese
¼ cup milk
1 teaspoon Dijon-style prepared mustard
1 envelope Lipton Golden Onion Recipe Soup Mix

Preheat oven to 375°.

In medium bowl, combine all ingredients; shape into
1-inch balls. On well greased baking sheet, arrange rice
balls and bake 20 minutes or until golden. Serve warm
and, if desired, with assorted mustards.

Makes about 2 dozen rice balls

❖ TIROPITAS

1 envelope Lipton Golden Onion Recipe Soup Mix
1 container (15 ounces) ricotta or creamed cottage
    cheese
3 eggs, beaten
8 ounces feta cheese, crumbled
½ cup plain dry bread crumbs
1 tablespoon snipped fresh dill
28 phyllo strudel sheets*
¾ cup butter or margarine, melted

Preheat oven to 425°.

In medium bowl, combine golden onion recipe soup
mix, ricotta, eggs, feta cheese, bread crumbs and dill;
set aside.

Unfold phyllo strudel sheets; cover with wax paper, then
damp cloth. Using 2 sheets at a time, brush lightly with
melted butter; cut sheet lengthwise into 4 equal strips.
Place 1 tablespoon cheese mixture on top corner of
each strip; fold corner over to opposite edge, forming a
triangle. Continue folding, keeping triangular shape
with each fold, until rolled completely to end. Arrange
on ungreased baking sheets; repeat with remaining
phyllo. Bake 20 minutes or until golden.

Makes about 5 dozen tiropitas

*Substitution: Use 3 packages (8 ounces each)
refrigerated crescent rolls. Separate dough according to
package directions. Cut each triangle in half and flatten
slightly. Place 1 tablespoon mixture in center of dough
and fold over sides, forming a triangle. Arrange on
ungreased baking sheets. Bake according to package
directions.

Spinach Rice Balls
Tiropitas

❖ BAKED STUFFED CLAMS

12 clams, well scrubbed*
    Water
1 envelope Lipton Vegetable Recipe Soup Mix
2 cups fresh bread crumbs
1 teaspoon oregano
⅛ teaspoon pepper
2 tablespoons oil
2 tablespoons grated Parmesan cheese

In large skillet, arrange clams, then add ½ inch water.
Cook covered over medium-high heat 5 minutes or
until clams open. Remove clams, reserving ¾ cup
liquid; strain liquid. (Discard any unopened clams.)
Remove clams from shells, then chop clams; reserve 12
shell halves.

Preheat oven to 350°. In small bowl, combine vegetable
recipe soup mix, bread crumbs, oregano and pepper.
Stir in clams and reserved liquid. Stuff reserved shells
with clam mixture. Arrange on baking sheet; drizzle
with oil, then sprinkle with cheese. Bake 15 minutes or
until golden.   *Makes 12 stuffed clams*

*Substitution: Use 2 cans (6½ ounces each) minced or
chopped clams, drained (reserve ¼ cup liquid). Mix
reserved liquid with ½ cup water. Shells can be
purchased separately.

MICROWAVE DIRECTIONS: Omit oil. Cook and stuff
clams as above. On plate, arrange clams and heat
uncovered at HIGH (Full Power) 5 minutes or until
heated through, rearranging clams once.

❖ STUFFED BROCCOLI 'N CHEESE ROLLS

1 package (10 ounces) frozen chopped broccoli,
    cooked and well drained
1 cup fresh or canned sliced mushrooms
1 cup shredded Cheddar cheese (about 4 ounces)
2 eggs, slightly beaten
1 envelope Lipton Vegetable Recipe Soup Mix
2 loaves (1 pound each) frozen bread dough,
    thawed
    Olive or vegetable oil

Preheat oven to 375°.

In medium bowl, combine broccoli, mushrooms,
cheese, eggs and vegetable recipe soup mix; set aside.

On lightly floured board, roll each bread loaf into a
10 × 7-inch rectangle. Spread ½ broccoli mixture over
each rectangle, leaving ½-inch border. Roll, starting at
long end, jelly-roll style; pinch ends to seal. Place seam
side down on lightly greased baking sheet, then brush
lightly with oil. Bake 45 minutes or until golden brown.
Slice and serve warm.

Makes 2 loaves, about 8 slices each

❖ SPICED MIXED NUTS

3 tablespoons butter or margarine
1 envelope Lipton Golden Onion Recipe Soup Mix
1/4 cup sugar
1 teaspoon ground cumin (optional)
1 jar (8 ounces) unsalted dry roasted mixed nuts

In large skillet, melt butter and stir in golden onion recipe soup mix thoroughly blended with sugar and cumin. Add nuts and cook over medium heat, stirring constantly, 5 minutes or until nuts are thoroughly coated with soup mixture and golden brown. Serve warm or spread nuts on baking sheet to cool. Store in airtight container up to 2 weeks.

Makes 2 1/2 cups nuts

❖ SAVORY PINWHEEL SANDWICHES

2 loaves unsliced white or pumpernickel bread,
    each cut into 8 lengthwise slices
    Festive Fillings* (choose two)
2 cups Lipton California Dip (see page 7)

Trim crust from bread; with rolling pin, gently flatten each slice.

Evenly spread 1 Festive Filling on 8 bread slices; roll, starting at narrow end, jelly-roll style. Repeat with second Festive Filling on remaining bread slices. Wrap in plastic wrap or wax paper, then chill. To serve, cut into 1/4-inch slices.   *Makes about 80 sandwiches*

*Festive Fillings—
• **HAM AND CHEESE:** Use 1 cup of the California Dip. Top each prepared bread slice with 1 thin slice cooked ham, then 1 thin slice Swiss or American cheese. Place quartered dill pickle across one end of each bread slice; roll, starting at pickle end.

• **BLUE CHEESE WALNUT:** Combine 1 cup of the California Dip, 2 ounces crumbled blue cheese and 1/2 cup finely chopped walnuts.

• **FRUITY CURRY:** Combine 1 cup of the California Dip, 3/4 teaspoon curry powder, 1/2 cup raisins, 1/2 cup finely chopped apple and 1 tablespoon milk.

• **WINE, CHEESE 'N OLIVE:** Combine 1 cup of the California Dip, 3/4 cup shredded Cheddar cheese (about 3 ounces) and 2 tablespoons dry red wine. Place 3 pitted ripe olives across one end of each prepared bread slice; roll, starting at olive end.

FREEZING/THAWING DIRECTIONS: Prepare sandwiches as above. Tightly wrap each sandwich roll in plastic wrap or wax paper, then heavy-duty aluminum foil; freeze. To serve, partially thaw frozen rolls; unwrap and cut into 1/4-inch slices. Continue thawing at room temperature about 1 hour.

❖ CRISPY BAGEL CHIPS

1 envelope Lipton Golden Onion Recipe Soup Mix
1/2 cup butter or margarine, melted
1 teaspoon basil leaves
1/2 teaspoon oregano
1/4 teaspoon garlic powder
4 to 5 plain bagels, cut into 1/8-inch slices

Preheat oven to 250°.

In small bowl, thoroughly blend all ingredients except bagels; generously brush on both sides of bagel slices. On two ungreased baking sheets, arrange bagel slices and bake 50 minutes or until crisp and golden. Store in airtight container up to 1 week.

Makes about 28 chips

❖ NACHO FONDUE

1 envelope Lipton Nacho Cheese Recipe Soup Mix
1 1/2 cups water
2 tablespoons tomato paste
1 cup shredded Monterey Jack or fontina cheese
    (about 3 ounces)
1 clove garlic, halved
    Assorted Nacho Dippers*

In 1-quart saucepan, with wire whip or fork, thoroughly blend nacho cheese recipe soup mix, water and tomato paste. Bring to a boil, stirring frequently, then reduce heat and simmer covered, stirring occasionally, 3 minutes. Stir in cheese until melted. Rub inside of fondue pot or chafing dish with garlic, then pour in cheese mixture. Serve with Assorted Nacho Dippers.

Makes about 1 1/2 cups fondue

*Assorted Nacho Dippers: Use cooked chicken nuggets or mini meatballs, tortilla or corn chips, bread cubes or mushrooms.

MICROWAVE DIRECTIONS: Decrease water to 1 cup plus 2 tablespoons and cheese to 3/4 cup. In 1-quart casserole, with wire whip or fork, thoroughly blend nacho cheese recipe soup mix, water and tomato paste. Heat uncovered at HIGH (Full Power), stirring occasionally, 5 minutes. Stir in cheese until melted. Serve as above.

SHORTCUT TIP

Peel garlic cloves quickly and easily by placing on a cutting board and hitting firmly with the flat side of a large knife.

---

*Spiced Mixed Nuts
Crispy Bagel Chips*

Serve with plenty of napkins!

CHINESE-STYLE SPARERIBS

1/2 cup butter or margarine
1 medium clove garlic, finely chopped
1 envelope Lipton Onion, Onion-Mushroom, Beefy Mushroom or Beefy Onion Recipe Soup Mix
1 can (16 ounces) tomato puree
1/2 cup brown sugar
1/4 cup soy sauce
1/4 cup white vinegar
1/4 cup chili sauce
5 pounds spareribs, country-style or baby back ribs

Preheat oven to 375°.

In large saucepan, melt butter and cook garlic with onion recipe soup mix over medium heat until garlic is golden. Stir in tomato puree, sugar, soy sauce, vinegar and chili sauce. Bring to a boil, then simmer, stirring occasionally, 15 minutes.

Meanwhile, in large aluminum-foil-lined baking pan or on broiler rack, arrange spareribs meaty side up and bake 20 minutes. Brush spareribs generously with sauce, then continue baking, meaty side up, brushing occasionally with remaining sauce, 50 minutes or until spareribs are done.

Makes about 12 appetizer or 7 main-dish servings

❖ PARTY CHEESE PUFF RING

1 envelope Lipton Onion-Mushroom Recipe Soup Mix
1 cup milk
1/4 cup butter or margarine
1 cup all-purpose flour
4 eggs
1 cup shredded Swiss cheese (about 4 ounces)
2 tablespoons milk

Preheat oven to 375°.

In medium saucepan, blend onion-mushroom recipe soup mix with 1 cup milk. Add butter and bring just to the boiling point; stir in flour. Cook over low heat, stirring constantly, until mixture forms a ball. Remove from heat, then beat in eggs, one at a time, beating well after each addition. Stir in 3/4 cup cheese.

On greased and lightly floured baking sheet, drop mixture by heaping tablespoons into 12 mounds, slightly touching, to form large circle. Brush with 2 tablespoons milk, then top with remaining cheese. Bake 40 minutes or until golden. Serve hot.

Makes 12 appetizers

❖ BEER BATTER FRIED VEGGIES 'N THINGS

Oil
1 envelope Lipton Golden Onion Recipe Soup Mix
1 cup all-purpose flour
1 teaspoon baking powder
2 eggs
1/2 cup beer
1 tablespoon prepared mustard
Suggested Veggies 'n Things*

In deep-fat fryer, heat oil to 375°.

Meanwhile, in large bowl, beat golden onion recipe soup mix, flour, baking powder, eggs, beer and mustard until smooth and well blended. Let batter stand 10 minutes. Dip Suggested Veggies 'n Things into batter, then carefully drop into hot oil. Fry, turning once, until golden brown; drain on paper towels. Serve warm.

Makes about 4 cups veggies 'n things

*Suggested Veggies 'n Things: Use any of the following to equal 4 to 5 cups—broccoli florets, cauliflowerets, sliced mushrooms or zucchini, or chilled mozzarella sticks.

❖ CHEESE & NUT STUFFED BREAD SLICES

1 loaf Italian or French bread (about 16 inches long)
1 (8-ounce) *plus* 1 (3-ounce) package cream cheese, softened
4 tablespoons butter or margarine, softened
1 cup shredded Cheddar cheese (about 4 ounces)
1 envelope Lipton Vegetable Recipe Soup Mix
1/2 cup chopped walnuts

Trim ends of bread, then cut bread crosswise into 4 pieces. Hollow out center of each piece, leaving 1/2-inch shell; reserve shells (save bread for fresh bread crumbs).

With food processor or electric mixer, combine cream cheese with butter until smooth. Add Cheddar cheese, vegetable recipe soup mix and walnuts; process until blended. Pack into reserved shells. Wrap in plastic wrap or wax paper, then chill at least 4 hours. To serve, cut into 1/2-inch slices. *Makes about 2 dozen slices*

NOTE: Store any remaining cheese mixture, covered, in refrigerator and serve as a spread with assorted crackers.

Chinese-Style Spareribs

FIRST COURSES

❖ SCALLOPS IN CREAMY WINE SAUCE

2 tablespoons butter or margarine
1 small clove garlic, finely chopped
1 cup sliced mushrooms
1/4 cup dry white wine
1 envelope Lipton Onion or Golden Onion Recipe
    Soup Mix
1/8 teaspoon pepper
2 cups (1 pint) whipping or heavy cream
1/4 cup milk
1 teaspoon lemon juice
1 pound bay scallops
    Buttered bread crumbs (optional)

In medium skillet, melt butter and cook garlic with mushrooms over medium heat until mushrooms are tender. Add wine and simmer 5 minutes. Blend onion recipe soup mix, pepper, cream, milk and lemon juice; stir into wine mixture. Bring just to the boiling point over medium heat, then simmer, stirring occasionally, 5 minutes. Stir in scallops and simmer an additional 5 minutes or until scallops are tender and sauce is thickened. Top with bread crumbs and serve, if desired, with French or Italian bread.

Makes about 8 appetizer or 4 main-dish servings

❖ CHILLED CHICKEN KABOBS WITH APRICOTS

1 envelope Lipton Golden Onion Recipe Soup Mix
1/2 cup sour cream or plain yogurt
1/2 cup apricot preserves
1/2 teaspoon curry powder
1 pound boneless chicken breasts, cooked and cut
    into 1 1/2-inch pieces
1 cup unsalted peanuts, finely chopped
12 dried apricots, halved

In medium bowl, thoroughly blend golden onion recipe soup mix, sour cream, preserves and curry. Dip cooked chicken in sour cream mixture, then peanuts, coating well. Place on wax-paper-lined cookie sheet and chill 1 hour.

On 6-inch skewers, alternately thread apricots with chicken; chill. Serve with remaining sour cream mixture for dipping.

Makes about 8 appetizer or 4 main-dish servings

This Watercress Sauce is also terrific with vegetable dippers!

❖ SEAFOOD COCKTAILS WITH WATERCRESS SAUCE

1 large bunch watercress, stems removed (about 2
    cups loosely packed)*
1 small bunch parsley, stems removed (about 1
    cup loosely packed)*
1 medium clove garlic, finely chopped
1 envelope Lipton Golden Onion Recipe Soup Mix
1/2 pint (8 ounces) sour cream
1/4 cup mayonnaise
1/8 teaspoon pepper
    Suggested Seafood**

In food processor or blender, combine watercress, parsley and garlic until blended. Add golden onion recipe soup mix, sour cream, mayonnaise and pepper; process until smooth. Chill at least 2 hours. Serve with Suggested Seafood. Garnish as desired.

*Makes about 2 cups sauce
or about 8 appetizer servings*

*Variation: Omit watercress. Use 2 small bunches parsley, stems removed (about 2 cups loosely packed).

**Suggested Seafood: Use about 2 pounds cooked and chilled butterflied shrimp, scallops, crab claws and legs, lobster meat or clams.

HOW TO BUTTERFLY SHRIMP

1. Peel and devein shrimp.

2. With a small sharp knife, slice down back of shrimp, almost completely through.

3. Spread and flatten to form butterfly shape.

Seafood Cocktails with Watercress Sauce

❖ CREAMY TORTELLINI PRIMAVERA

3 tablespoons olive or vegetable oil
1 medium clove garlic, finely chopped
1 envelope Lipton Vegetable Recipe Soup Mix
2 cups (1 pint) light cream or half and half
1 pound egg or spinach tortellini, cooked and
    drained
¼ cup grated Parmesan cheese
¼ cup finely chopped parsley
¼ teaspoon pepper

In large skillet, heat oil and cook garlic over medium heat until golden. Stir in vegetable recipe soup mix blended with cream, then hot tortellini. Bring just to the boiling point, then simmer, stirring occasionally, 5 minutes. Stir in remaining ingredients. Garnish, if desired, with additional parsley and cheese.

Makes about 4 appetizer or 2 main-dish servings

MICROWAVE DIRECTIONS: In 2-quart casserole, heat oil with garlic at HIGH (Full Power) 2 minutes. Stir in vegetable recipe soup mix blended with cream and heat uncovered 4 minutes, stirring twice. Add hot tortellini and heat uncovered 3 minutes. Stir in remaining ingredients and heat 1 minute. Garnish and serve as above.

Creamy Tortellini Primavera

❖ HERB 'N ONION VINAIGRETTE DRESSING

¼ cup water
¼ cup red wine vinegar
1 envelope Lipton Golden Onion or Onion Recipe Soup Mix
1 tablespoon finely chopped parsley
2 tablespoons Dijon-style prepared mustard
1 medium clove garlic, finely chopped
½ cup vegetable or olive oil
Pepper to taste

In medium bowl, thoroughly blend water, vinegar, golden onion recipe soup mix, parsley, mustard and garlic. Slowly add oil, stirring constantly, until ingredients are well blended. Stir in pepper. Use as a dressing for your favorite greens. Store covered in refrigerator. *Makes about 1½ cups dressing*

NOTE: Some oils, such as olive oil, will congeal upon refrigeration; therefore, let dressing return to room temperature before serving.

QUICK CROUTONS

Add a gourmet touch to your salad while making use of day-old bread. Cut 3 slices of bread into ½-inch cubes. In medium skillet, heat 3 tablespoons oil with ¼ teaspoon garlic powder and cook bread cubes, stirring frequently, until bread is crisp and golden. Drain well on paper towels. *Makes about 1½ cups croutons.*

❖ VEGETABLE RICE SALAD CUPS

⅔ cup mayonnaise
½ cup Wish-Bone® Italian Dressing
1 tablespoon lemon juice
½ cup sliced green onions
2 tablespoons sesame seeds, toasted (optional)
1 tablespoon finely chopped parsley or coriander (cilantro)
1 envelope Lipton Vegetable Recipe Soup Mix
4 cups cooked rice
Lettuce leaves
1 can (15 ounces) ears of baby corn, drained

In large bowl, combine mayonnaise, dressing, lemon juice, green onions, sesame seeds, parsley and vegetable recipe soup mix. Stir in rice; chill. To serve, pack salad mixture into 5-ounce custard cups or bowls, then unmold onto lettuce-lined serving plates. Garnish with corn and, if desired, additional parsley.
Makes about 6 servings

❖ STUFFED MUSHROOMS WITH CRABMEAT

12 to 15 large mushrooms
1 envelope Lipton Vegetable Recipe Soup Mix
1 package (6 ounces) frozen crabmeat, thawed and squeezed dry
½ cup sour cream
3 tablespoons plain dry bread crumbs
1 tablespoon snipped fresh dill*
3 dashes hot pepper sauce
⅛ teaspoon pepper
2 tablespoons butter or margarine, melted

Preheat oven to 350°.

Remove and finely chop mushroom stems. In medium bowl, combine chopped mushroom stems, vegetable recipe soup mix, crabmeat, sour cream, bread crumbs, dill, hot pepper sauce and pepper; set aside.

On lightly greased baking sheet, arrange mushroom caps; stuff with crabmeat mixture, then brush with butter. Bake 15 minutes or until tender.
Makes about 12 appetizers

*Substitution: Use 1 teaspoon dried dill weed.

MAKE-AHEAD DIRECTIONS: Mushrooms can be partially prepared up to 1 day ahead. Simply prepare and stuff as above. Cover and refrigerate. To serve, brush with butter, then bake as above.

❖ PASTA DI PINA

3 tablespoons olive or vegetable oil
4 medium cloves garlic, finely chopped
2 tablespoons fresh bread crumbs
⅛ teaspoon pepper
1 envelope Lipton Golden Onion Recipe Soup Mix
3½ cups water
6 ounces uncooked fine egg noodles
2 tablespoons finely chopped parsley
Grated Parmesan cheese

In medium skillet, heat oil and cook garlic with bread crumbs over medium heat, stirring constantly, until garlic and bread crumbs are golden. Stir in pepper; set aside.

In large saucepan, thoroughly blend golden onion recipe soup mix with water. Bring to a boil, then stir in uncooked noodles. Simmer uncovered, stirring frequently, 7 minutes or until noodles are tender (DO NOT DRAIN). Remove from heat, then toss with bread crumb mixture and parsley. Sprinkle with cheese.
Makes about 4 appetizer or 2 main-dish servings

SOUP'S ON

SOUPS FOR SUPPER

❖ HOMESTYLE CHICKEN SOUP

1 envelope Lipton Golden Onion Recipe Soup Mix
5 cups water
2 1/2- to 3-pound chicken, cut into 8 pieces and skinned
2 medium carrots, coarsely chopped
1 large stalk celery, coarsely chopped
1 teaspoon thyme leaves
3 peppercorns
1 bay leaf (optional)
1/2 cup uncooked regular rice*

In large saucepan or stockpot, thoroughly blend golden onion recipe soup mix with water. Add chicken, carrots, celery, thyme, peppercorns and bay leaf. Bring to a boil, then simmer covered 45 minutes or until chicken is done. Remove chicken and bay leaf; cool slightly. Remove meat from chicken bones and cut into bite-size pieces; set aside.

Meanwhile, bring soup mixture to a boil and stir in uncooked rice. Reduce heat and simmer covered 20 minutes or until rice is tender. Return chicken meat to soup mixture and heat through.

Makes about 4 (1 3/4-cup) servings

*Substitution: Use 1/3 cup egg pastina.

SOUPS ON THE SIDE

You can also enjoy any of these hearty soup recipes in the "Soups for Supper" section as a first course or as an accompaniment to a meal. Simply serve a 1-cup portion instead of the main-dish serving size suggested.

❖ LENTIL AND BROWN RICE SOUP

1 envelope Lipton Onion, Beefy Onion or Beefy Mushroom Recipe Soup Mix
4 cups water
3/4 cup lentils, rinsed and drained
1/2 cup uncooked brown or regular rice
1 can (14 1/2 ounces) whole peeled tomatoes, undrained and coarsely chopped
1 medium carrot, coarsely chopped
1 large stalk celery, coarsely chopped
1/2 teaspoon basil leaves
1/2 teaspoon oregano
1/4 teaspoon thyme leaves (optional)
1 tablespoon finely chopped parsley
1 tablespoon apple cider vinegar
1/4 teaspoon pepper

In large saucepan or stockpot, combine onion recipe soup mix, water, lentils, uncooked rice, tomatoes, carrot, celery, basil, oregano and thyme. Bring to a boil, then simmer covered, stirring occasionally, 45 minutes or until lentils and rice are tender. Stir in remaining ingredients. *Makes about 3 (2-cup) servings*

MICROWAVE DIRECTIONS: In 3-quart casserole, combine onion recipe soup mix, water, tomatoes, carrot, celery, basil, oregano and thyme. Heat covered at HIGH (Full Power) 12 minutes or until boiling. Stir in lentils and uncooked brown rice* and heat covered at MEDIUM (50% Full Power), stirring occasionally, 60 minutes or until lentils and rice are tender. Stir in remaining ingredients. Let stand covered 5 minutes.

*If using uncooked regular rice, decrease 60-minute cook time to 30 minutes.

Lentil and Brown Rice Soup

❖ FISHERMAN'S BOUILLABAISSE

¼ cup olive or vegetable oil
2 cloves garlic, finely chopped
1 cup water
½ cup dry white wine
1 envelope Lipton Onion or Onion-Mushroom
   Recipe Soup Mix
1 tablespoon finely chopped parsley
1 teaspoon thyme leaves
1 can (14½ ounces) whole peeled tomatoes,
   undrained and chopped
3 lobster tails (about 1½ pounds), cut into 3-inch
   pieces
1 pound red snapper, cod, halibut or haddock, cut
   into pieces
6 clams, well scrubbed
6 mussels, well scrubbed

In large saucepan or stockpot, heat oil and cook garlic over medium heat until golden. Add water, wine, onion recipe soup mix, parsley and thyme; blend thoroughly. Stir in tomatoes. Bring to a boil, then simmer covered 15 minutes. Add lobster and snapper and simmer 10 minutes. Add clams and mussels and simmer an additional 5 minutes or until shells open. (Discard any unopened shells.) Serve, if desired, with bread or rolls.

Makes about 4 (2-cup) servings

❖ HEARTY MEATLESS CHILI

1 envelope Lipton Onion, Onion-Mushroom or
   Beefy Mushroom Recipe Soup Mix
4 cups water
1 can (16 ounces) chick peas or garbanzos, rinsed
   and drained
1 can (16 ounces) red kidney beans, rinsed and
   drained
1 can (14½ ounces) whole peeled tomatoes,
   undrained and chopped
1 cup lentils, rinsed and drained
1 large stalk celery, coarsely chopped
1 tablespoon chili powder
2 teaspoons ground cumin
1 medium clove garlic, finely chopped
¼ teaspoon crushed red pepper

In large saucepan or stockpot, combine all ingredients. Bring to a boil, then simmer covered, stirring occasionally, 20 minutes or until lentils are almost tender. Remove cover and simmer, stirring occasionally, an additional 30 minutes or until liquid is almost absorbed and lentils are tender. Serve, if desired, over hot cooked brown or white rice and top with shredded Cheddar cheese. *Makes about 4 (2-cup) servings*

❖ HEARTY SHRIMP GUMBO

¼ cup oil
¼ cup all-purpose flour
1 large stalk celery, coarsely chopped
1 small green pepper, coarsely chopped
2 medium cloves garlic, finely chopped
1 envelope Lipton Onion or Onion-Mushroom
   Recipe Soup Mix
4 cups water
1 can (14½ ounces) whole peeled tomatoes,
   undrained and chopped
1 package (10 ounces) frozen whole baby okra,
   thawed and cut into 1-inch pieces
1 teaspoon ground cumin
1 teaspoon thyme leaves
¼ teaspoon hot pepper sauce
1 bay leaf (optional)
1 pound uncooked medium shrimp, cleaned
1 tablespoon finely chopped parsley
   Salt and pepper to taste
   Hot cooked rice

In large saucepan or stockpot, heat oil and cook flour over medium-high heat, stirring constantly, 10 minutes or until deep reddish brown. Stir in celery, green pepper and garlic. Cook, stirring occasionally, 6 minutes or until vegetables are tender. Stir in onion recipe soup mix, water, tomatoes, okra, cumin, thyme, hot pepper sauce and bay leaf. Bring to a boil, then simmer uncovered, stirring occasionally, 40 minutes. Stir in shrimp, parsley, salt and pepper. Simmer an additional 5 minutes or until shrimp are done. Remove bay leaf. Serve over hot rice.

Makes about 4 (2-cup) servings

Fisherman's Bouillabaisse

❖ CRISPY POTATO SKIN CROUTONS

1 envelope Lipton Golden Onion or Onion Recipe Soup Mix
1/2 cup butter or margarine, softened
8 medium potatoes (about 3 1/2 pounds), unpeeled and baked*

Preheat oven to 450°.

In small bowl, thoroughly blend golden onion recipe soup mix with butter; set aside.

Cut potatoes in half lengthwise. Remove pulp, leaving 1/4-inch shell (save pulp for another use); cut shells into 8 pieces. Arrange on ungreased baking sheet and brush generously with butter mixture. Bake 20 minutes or until crisp and golden brown. Serve on your favorite soup or enjoy as a snack.   *Makes about 64 croutons*

*Potatoes can also be cooked in the microwave oven.

❖ BLACK BEAN SOUP

4 quarts water
1 pound dried black beans, rinsed and drained
1 envelope Lipton Onion Recipe Soup Mix
1 small ham hock or bone
2 stalks celery, chopped
2 cloves garlic, chopped
1 teaspoon lemon juice
1 whole clove
1 bay leaf
  Few sprigs parsley
3 tablespoons sherry
1 teaspoon pepper

In large saucepan or stockpot, bring 2 quarts water to a boil; add beans and boil 2 minutes. Remove from heat, then let stand covered 1 hour; drain.

In large saucepan or stockpot, combine beans, remaining water, onion recipe soup mix, ham hock, celery, garlic, lemon juice, clove, bay leaf and parsley. Bring to a boil, then simmer covered, stirring occasionally, 3 hours or until beans are tender.

Remove ham hock and bay leaf. In food processor or blender, puree hot soup mixture, adding water if too thick, then return to saucepan. Bring to a boil, then stir in sherry and pepper. Garnish, if desired, with sour cream, lemon slices or hard-cooked egg.
Makes about 4 (2-cup) servings

❖ CORNED BEEF & CABBAGE CHOWDER

2 tablespoons butter or margarine
1/2 cup thinly sliced celery
1/2 cup finely chopped onion
2 cups water
2 cups coarsely shredded cabbage
1 cup thinly sliced carrots
1 envelope Lipton Noodle Soup Mix with Real Chicken Broth
1 teaspoon dry mustard
1 1/2 tablespoons all-purpose flour
2 cups milk
1/4 pound thinly sliced cooked corned beef, cut into thin strips

In large saucepan or stockpot, melt butter and cook celery and onion over medium heat until tender. Stir in water, cabbage and carrots. Bring to a boil, then simmer covered, stirring occasionally, 15 minutes or until vegetables are almost tender. Stir in noodle soup mix, then mustard and flour blended with milk. Bring just to the boiling point, then simmer, stirring constantly, until chowder is thickened, about 5 minutes. Stir in corned beef and heat through, but do not boil.
Makes about 3 (1 3/4-cup) servings

MICROWAVE DIRECTIONS: In 3-quart casserole, heat butter at HIGH (Full Power) 1 minute. Add celery and onion and heat 5 minutes or until vegetables are tender, stirring once. Add water, cabbage and carrots. Heat covered, stirring occasionally, 15 minutes or until vegetables are tender. Stir in noodle soup mix, then mustard and flour blended with milk. Heat covered, stirring occasionally, 7 minutes or until chowder is thickened. Stir in corned beef. Let stand covered 5 minutes.

❖ OLD-FASHIONED BRUNSWICK STEW

1 envelope Lipton Golden Onion Recipe Soup Mix
4 cups water
2 large potatoes, peeled and diced
2 cups sliced fresh or frozen okra
1 can (17 ounces) cream-style corn, undrained
1 can (14 1/2 ounces) whole peeled tomatoes, undrained and chopped
1 teaspoon rosemary leaves
1 bay leaf (optional)
2 cups cut-up cooked chicken
  Salt and pepper to taste

In large saucepan or stockpot, thoroughly blend golden onion recipe soup mix with water. Add potatoes, okra, corn, tomatoes, rosemary and bay leaf. Bring to a boil, then simmer covered, stirring occasionally, 40 minutes or until vegetables are tender. Stir in remaining ingredients and heat through. Remove bay leaf.
Makes about 4 (2-cup) servings

BRING ON THE SOUP

✤ CHILLY CUCUMBER SOUP

- 2 tablespoons butter or margarine
- 2 tablespoons all-purpose flour
- 4 large cucumbers, peeled, seeded and finely chopped (about 3¹/₂ cups)
- ¹/₄ cup finely chopped parsley
- ¹/₄ cup finely chopped celery leaves
- 1 envelope Lipton Golden Onion Recipe Soup Mix
- 2 cups water
- 2 cups (1 pint) light cream or half and half

In large saucepan, melt butter and cook flour over medium heat, stirring constantly, 3 minutes. Add cucumbers, parsley and celery leaves. Reduce heat to low and cook 8 minutes or until vegetables are tender. Stir in golden onion recipe soup mix thoroughly blended with water. Bring to a boil, then simmer covered 15 minutes. Remove from heat, then cool.

In food processor or blender, puree soup mixture. Stir in cream; chill. Serve cold and garnish, if desired, with cucumber slices and lemon peel.

Makes about 6 (1-cup) servings

Chilly Cucumber Soup

❖ COUNTRY CORN CHOWDER

    2 tablespoons butter or margarine
 1/2 cup chopped celery
    2 cups diced potatoes (about 2 medium)
    1 envelope Lipton Golden Onion Recipe Soup Mix
 2 1/2 cups water
    1 can (17 ounces) whole kernel corn, drained
    1 cup milk
 1/4 teaspoon pepper
    Salt to taste

In large saucepan or stockpot, melt butter and cook celery over medium heat until tender. Stir in potatoes, then golden onion recipe soup mix thoroughly blended with water. Bring to a boil, then simmer 15 minutes or until potatoes are tender. Stir in corn, milk and pepper.

In food processor or blender, puree hot soup mixture, then return to saucepan. Stir in salt and heat through.
Makes about 6 (1-cup) servings

MICROWAVE DIRECTIONS: In 2-quart casserole, heat butter at HIGH (Full Power) 1 minute. Add celery and heat uncovered 3 minutes or until tender. Stir in potatoes, then golden onion recipe soup mix thoroughly blended with water. Heat covered 15 minutes or until potatoes are tender, stirring once. Stir in corn, milk and pepper. Puree mixture as above, then return to casserole. Stir in salt and heat uncovered 4 minutes or until heated through.

❖ CREAMY CAULIFLOWER AU GRATIN SOUP

    1 envelope Lipton Golden Onion Recipe Soup Mix
    3 cups water
    3 cups medium cauliflowerets
    1 large stalk celery, coarsely chopped
 1/2 cup light cream or half and half
 3/4 cup shredded Cheddar cheese (about 3 1/2 ounces)
 1/4 teaspoon pepper

In medium saucepan, thoroughly blend golden onion recipe soup mix with water. Add cauliflowerets and celery. Bring to a boil, then simmer covered, stirring occasionally, 20 minutes or until vegetables are tender.

In food processor or blender, puree hot soup mixture, then return to saucepan. Stir in remaining ingredients. Simmer, stirring occasionally, 5 minutes or until cheese is melted.   *Makes about 5 (1-cup) servings*

MICROWAVE DIRECTIONS: In 2-quart casserole, thoroughly blend golden onion recipe soup mix with water. Add cauliflowerets and celery. Heat covered at HIGH (Full Power) 20 minutes or until cauliflowerets are tender, stirring once. Puree as above; return to casserole. Add remaining ingredients and stir until cheese is melted. Let stand covered 5 minutes.

❖ CHUNKY CHICKEN NOODLE SOUP WITH VEGETABLES

    2 envelopes Lipton Noodle Soup Mix with Real
        Chicken Broth
    6 cups water
 1/2 small head escarole, torn into pieces (about
        2 cups)*
    1 large stalk celery, sliced
    1 small carrot, sliced
 1/4 cup frozen peas (optional)
    1 small clove garlic, finely chopped
 1/2 teaspoon thyme leaves
    2 whole cloves
    1 bay leaf
    2 cups cut-up cooked chicken
    1 tablespoon finely chopped parsley

In large saucepan or stockpot, combine noodle soup mix, water, escarole, celery, carrot, peas, garlic, thyme, cloves and bay leaf. Bring to a boil, then simmer uncovered, stirring occasionally, 15 minutes or until vegetables are tender. Stir in chicken and parsley and heat through. Remove bay leaf.
Makes about 7 (1-cup) servings

*Substitution: Use 2 cups shredded cabbage.

MICROWAVE DIRECTIONS: In 3-quart casserole, combine as above. Heat uncovered at HIGH (Full Power), stirring occasionally, 20 minutes or until vegetables are tender. Stir in chicken and parsley and heat uncovered 1 minute or until heated through. Remove bay leaf. Let stand covered 5 minutes.

> ### *PLAN-AHEAD TIP*
>
> Cook up a storm on weekends for "thaw and heat" weekday dinners. Freeze soups, stocks, meat loaf and baked goods, then simply defrost and heat for a speedy supper.

Chunky Chicken Noodle Soup with Vegetables

❖ WISCONSIN CHEESE 'N BEER SOUP

2 tablespoons butter or margarine
2 tablespoons all-purpose flour
1 envelope Lipton Golden Onion Recipe Soup Mix
3 cups milk
1 teaspoon Worcestershire sauce
1 cup shredded Cheddar cheese (about 4 ounces)
1/2 cup beer
1 teaspoon prepared mustard

In medium saucepan, melt butter and cook flour over medium heat, stirring constantly, 3 minutes or until bubbling. Stir in golden onion recipe soup mix thoroughly blended with milk and Worcestershire sauce. Bring just to the boiling point, then simmer, stirring occasionally, 10 minutes. Stir in remaining ingredients and simmer, stirring constantly, 5 minutes or until cheese is melted. Garnish, if desired, with additional cheese, chopped red pepper and parsley.

Makes about 4 (1-cup) servings

❖ COUNTRY ITALIAN SOUP

1 tablespoon oil
1/2 pound boneless beef, cut into 1-inch cubes
1 can (14 1/2 ounces) whole peeled tomatoes, undrained and chopped
1 envelope Lipton Onion or Beefy Mushroom Recipe Soup Mix
3 cups water
1 medium onion, cut into chunks
1 large stalk celery, cut into 1-inch pieces
1/2 cup sliced carrot
1 cup cut green beans
1 can (16 ounces) chick peas or garbanzos, rinsed and drained
1/2 cup sliced zucchini
1/4 cup uncooked elbow macaroni
1/4 teaspoon oregano

In large saucepan or stockpot, heat oil and brown beef over medium-high heat. Add tomatoes, then onion recipe soup mix blended with water. Simmer uncovered, stirring occasionally, 30 minutes. Add onion, celery, carrot and green beans. Simmer uncovered, stirring occasionally, 30 minutes. Stir in remaining ingredients and simmer uncovered, stirring occasionally, an additional 15 minutes or until vegetables and macaroni are tender. Serve, if desired, with grated Parmesan cheese.

Makes about 8 (1-cup) servings

❖ GREEN AND YELLOW SQUASH SOUP

1 envelope Lipton Golden Onion Recipe Soup Mix
3 cups water
1 large zucchini, sliced (about 1 1/2 cups)
1 large yellow squash, sliced (about 1 1/2 cups)
1/4 cup loosely packed fresh basil leaves*
Pepper to taste

In large saucepan, thoroughly blend golden onion recipe soup mix with water. Add remaining ingredients. Bring to a boil, then simmer uncovered, stirring occasionally, 15 minutes or until vegetables are tender.

In food processor or blender, puree hot soup mixture. Serve hot or chilled. *Makes about 5 (1-cup) servings*

*Substitution: Use 1 tablespoon dried basil leaves.

MICROWAVE DIRECTIONS: In 2-quart casserole, thoroughly blend golden onion recipe soup mix with water. Add remaining ingredients. Heat covered at HIGH (Full Power) 8 minutes or until boiling. Remove cover and heat an additional 7 minutes or until vegetables are tender, stirring once. Puree and serve as above.

❖ ORIENTAL-STYLE CHICKEN SOUP

1 envelope Lipton Chicken Noodle Soup Mix with Diced White Chicken Meat
4 cups water
4 ounces snow peas (about 1 cup)
1/2 cup bamboo shoots
1 can (8 ounces) water chestnuts, drained and sliced
1 tablespoon brown sugar
1 tablespoon apple cider vinegar
2 teaspoons soy sauce
1/4 teaspoon ground ginger
8 ounces cooked lean boneless pork, cut into thin strips
1 tablespoon chopped pimiento

In large saucepan or stockpot, combine chicken noodle soup mix, water, snow peas, bamboo shoots, water chestnuts, sugar, vinegar, soy sauce and ginger. Bring to a boil, then simmer uncovered 5 minutes. Add pork and pimiento and heat through.

Makes about 6 (1-cup) servings

MICROWAVE DIRECTIONS: In 3-quart casserole, heat water, uncovered, at HIGH (Full Power) 6 minutes or until boiling. Stir in chicken noodle soup mix, snow peas, bamboo shoots, water chestnuts, sugar, vinegar, soy sauce and ginger. Heat uncovered 8 minutes, stirring once. Stir in pork and pimiento and heat uncovered 2 minutes or until vegetables are tender. Let stand covered 5 minutes.

Wisconsin Cheese 'n Beer Soup

ON-THE-SIDE

❖ HOMESTYLE ZUCCHINI & TOMATOES

2 tablespoons oil
1 medium clove garlic, finely chopped*
3 medium zucchini, thinly sliced (about 4½ cups)
1 can (14½ ounces) whole peeled tomatoes, drained and chopped (reserve liquid)
1 envelope Lipton Golden Onion or Onion Recipe Soup Mix
½ teaspoon basil leaves

In large skillet, heat oil and cook garlic with zucchini over medium-high heat 3 minutes. Stir in tomatoes, then golden onion recipe soup mix thoroughly blended with reserved liquid and basil. Bring to a boil, then simmer, stirring occasionally, 10 minutes or until zucchini is tender and sauce is slightly thickened.

Makes about 4 servings

*Substitution: Use ¼ teaspoon garlic powder.

MICROWAVE DIRECTIONS: In 2-quart casserole, combine zucchini with tomatoes. Stir in golden onion recipe soup mix thoroughly blended with reserved liquid, garlic and basil. Heat covered at HIGH (Full Power) 5 minutes, stirring once. Remove cover and heat 4 minutes or until zucchini is tender, stirring once. Let stand covered 2 minutes.

❖ "SOUPER" ORIENTAL RICE

1 envelope Lipton Vegetable Recipe Soup Mix
2¾ cups water
2 tablespoons butter or margarine
1½ tablespoons soy sauce
¼ teaspoon ground ginger
1 cup uncooked regular rice

In medium saucepan, combine all ingredients except rice; bring to a boil. Stir in uncooked rice and simmer covered 20 minutes or until rice is tender.

Makes about 6 servings

❖ ONION-BUTTERED JULIENNE VEGETABLES

In large skillet, melt ¼ cup Lipton Onion Butter (see page 69) and cook 4 cups julienne-cut vegetables (any combination of carrots, celery, turnips or zucchini), covered over medium heat, stirring occasionally, until tender.

Makes about 4 servings

MICROWAVE DIRECTIONS: In 2-quart oblong baking dish, heat vegetables with Onion Butter, covered, at HIGH (Full Power), stirring occasionally, 7 minutes or until tender.

❖ TATER 'N APPLE BAKE

½ cup Lipton Onion Butter (see page 69)
½ cup brown sugar
⅓ cup coarsely chopped walnuts
1 teaspoon ground cinnamon
4 cups sliced cooked sweet potatoes or yams (about 4 medium)
3 cups sliced apples
2 tablespoons Lipton Onion Butter

Preheat oven to 375°.

In small bowl, blend ½ cup Lipton Onion Butter, sugar, walnuts and cinnamon.

In greased 2-quart casserole, layer ⅓ potatoes, ⅓ apples and ½ onion butter mixture; repeat. Arrange remaining ⅓ potatoes and apples, then 2 tablespoons Onion Butter. Bake covered 30 minutes or until apples are tender. Garnish, if desired, with additional walnuts.

Makes about 8 servings

MICROWAVE DIRECTIONS: Prepare casserole as above. Heat covered at HIGH (Full Power), turning casserole occasionally, 12 minutes or until apples are tender. Let stand covered 5 minutes. Garnish as above.

Homestyle Zucchini & Tomatoes

✤ SPAGHETTI SQUASH TOSS

2 tablespoons butter or margarine
1 cup sliced mushrooms
1 envelope Lipton Vegetable Recipe Soup Mix
1 cup (½ pint) light cream or half and half
¼ cup dry white wine
½ medium spaghetti squash, seeded and cooked
2 tablespoons grated Parmesan cheese

In large saucepan, melt butter and cook mushrooms over medium heat until tender. Stir in vegetable recipe soup mix blended with cream and wine. Bring just to the boiling point, then simmer, stirring occasionally, 5 minutes or until sauce is thickened.

Meanwhile, with fork, gently remove spaghetti-like strands from squash. Add squash and cheese to saucepan; toss well. Serve, if desired, with additional cheese and freshly ground pepper.

Makes about 4 servings

NOTE: Recipe can be doubled.

MICROWAVE DIRECTIONS: In 1½-quart casserole, heat butter with mushrooms, uncovered, at HIGH (Full Power) 2 minutes. Stir in vegetable recipe soup mix blended with cream and wine. Heat uncovered 5 minutes or until sauce is thickened, stirring once. Meanwhile, prepare squash as above. Add squash and cheese to casserole and heat uncovered 1 minute or until heated through. Let stand covered 5 minutes. Serve as above.

EASY SQUASH COOKERY

Pierce squash with fork, then cook according to one of the following methods:

● Bake whole squash at 350°, 1 to 1½ hours or until fork-tender.

● Place whole squash in large saucepan or stockpot; add water to cover. Boil 35 to 45 minutes or until fork-tender.

● Cut squash in half. In oblong baking dish, place squash, cut side down, and microwave at HIGH (Full Power), turning dish occasionally, 17 minutes or until fork-tender.

✤ COUNTRY WILD RICE WITH ALMONDS

1 envelope Lipton Onion Recipe Soup Mix
3 cups water
1 cup uncooked wild rice
2 cups hot cooked white rice
½ cup golden or dark raisins (optional)
½ cup slivered almonds, toasted
2 tablespoons finely chopped parsley or coriander (cilantro)
¼ cup butter or margarine

In large saucepan, blend onion recipe soup mix with water; bring to a boil. Stir in uncooked wild rice and cook covered at a slow boil 50 minutes or until water is absorbed and rice kernels appear split. Add remaining ingredients and toss well. *Makes about 12 servings*

✤ NACHO CHEESE SAUCE

In 1-quart saucepan, with wire whip or fork, thoroughly blend 1 envelope Lipton Nacho Cheese Recipe Soup Mix with 1½ cups milk. Bring just to the boiling point, stirring frequently, then reduce heat and simmer covered, stirring occasionally, 5 minutes. Serve over hamburgers, steak sandwiches, tacos or tortilla chips. *Makes about 1½ cups sauce*

MICROWAVE DIRECTIONS: Decrease milk to 1¼ cups. In 1½-quart casserole, with wire whip or fork, thoroughly blend nacho cheese recipe soup mix with milk. Heat uncovered at HIGH (Full Power), stirring occasionally, 6 minutes.

✤ ONION-HERB BAKED BREAD

1 envelope Lipton Golden Onion Recipe Soup Mix
1 medium clove garlic, finely chopped
1 teaspoon basil leaves
1 teaspoon oregano
⅛ teaspoon pepper
½ cup butter or margarine, softened
1 loaf Italian or French bread (about 16 inches long), halved lengthwise

Preheat oven to 375°.

In small bowl, thoroughly blend all ingredients except bread; generously spread on bread halves. On baking sheet, arrange bread, cut side up, and bake 15 minutes or until golden. Serve warm. *Makes 1 loaf*

NOTE: Store any remaining spread, covered, in refrigerator for future use.

Spaghetti Squash Toss

✤ ONION-MUSHROOM GRAVY

1 envelope Lipton Onion-Mushroom Recipe Soup
    Mix
1²/3 cups water
1¹/2 tablespoons all-purpose flour

In medium saucepan, blend onion-mushroom recipe
soup mix with 1¹/3 cups water. Bring to a boil, then
simmer covered, stirring occasionally, 8 minutes. Stir in
flour blended with remaining water. Bring to a boil,
then simmer, stirring constantly, until gravy is
thickened, about 2 minutes.

Makes about 1¹/2 cups gravy

MICROWAVE DIRECTIONS: In 1-quart casserole,
blend onion-mushroom recipe soup mix with 1¹/3 cups
water. Heat uncovered at HIGH (Full Power), stirring
occasionally, 5 minutes. Stir in flour blended with
remaining water. Heat, stirring occasionally, 5 minutes
or until gravy is thickened. Let stand covered 5
minutes.

✤ BEEFY MUSHROOM GRAVY

1 envelope Lipton Beefy Mushroom Recipe Soup
    Mix
1³/4 cups water
1 tablespoon all-purpose flour

In medium saucepan, blend beefy mushroom recipe
soup mix with 1¹/4 cups water. Bring to a boil, then
simmer covered, stirring occasionally, 8 minutes. Stir in
flour blended with remaining water. Bring to a boil,
then simmer, stirring constantly, until gravy is
thickened, about 2 minutes.

Makes about 1¹/2 cups gravy

MICROWAVE DIRECTIONS: Increase water to 2 cups.
In 1-quart casserole, blend beefy mushroom recipe
soup mix with 1¹/2 cups water. Heat uncovered at HIGH
(Full Power), stirring occasionally, 5 minutes. Stir in
flour blended with remaining ¹/2 cup water. Heat,
stirring occasionally, 5 minutes or until gravy is
thickened. Let stand covered 5 minutes.

DELICIOUS GRAVY VARIATIONS

Blend **with** soup mix and water, then continue as
directed:

- 3 tablespoons dry red wine

- ¹/2 to 1 tablespoon lemon juice and 1
tablespoon finely chopped parsley

- 1 tablespoon tomato paste and ¹/4 to ¹/2
teaspoon basil leaves

✤ ONION GRAVY

1 envelope Lipton Onion Recipe Soup Mix
2 cups water
2 tablespoons all-purpose flour

In medium saucepan, blend onion recipe soup mix
with 1¹/2 cups water. Bring to a boil, then simmer
covered, stirring occasionally, 8 minutes. Stir in flour
blended with remaining water. Bring to a boil, then
simmer, stirring constantly, until gravy is thickened,
about 2 minutes.   *Makes about 1³/4 cups gravy*

MICROWAVE DIRECTIONS: In 1-quart casserole,
blend onion recipe soup mix with 1¹/2 cups water. Heat
uncovered at HIGH (Full Power), stirring occasionally, 5
minutes. Stir in flour blended with remaining water.
Heat, stirring occasionally, 5 minutes or until gravy is
thickened. Let stand covered 5 minutes.

✤ BEEFY ONION GRAVY

1 envelope Lipton Beefy Onion Recipe Soup Mix
1³/4 cups water
2 tablespoons all-purpose flour

In medium saucepan, blend beefy onion recipe soup
mix with 1¹/4 cups water. Bring to a boil, then simmer
covered, stirring occasionally, 8 minutes. Stir in flour
blended with remaining water. Bring to a boil, then
simmer, stirring constantly, until gravy is thickened,
about 2 minutes.   *Makes about 1¹/2 cups gravy*

MICROWAVE DIRECTIONS: In 1-quart casserole,
blend beefy onion recipe soup mix with 1¹/4 cups water.
Heat uncovered at HIGH (Full Power), stirring
occasionally, 5 minutes. Stir in flour blended with
remaining water. Heat, stirring occasionally, 5 minutes
or until gravy is thickened. Let stand 5 minutes.

✤ CREAMY HERB SAUCE

In 1-quart saucepan, with wire whip or fork, thoroughly
blend 1 envelope Lipton Creamy Herb Recipe Soup Mix
with 2 cups milk. Bring just to the boiling point,
stirring frequently, then reduce heat and simmer,
stirring occasionally, 5 minutes. Serve over hot cooked
chicken, cauliflower, broccoli or fish fillets.

Makes about 2 cups sauce

MICROWAVE DIRECTIONS: Decrease milk to 1¹/2
cups. In 1¹/2-quart casserole, with wire whip or fork,
thoroughly blend creamy herb recipe soup mix with
milk. Heat uncovered at HIGH (Full Power), stirring
occasionally, 6 minutes.

❖ CRISP ONION-ROASTED POTATOES

1 envelope Lipton Onion or Onion-Mushroom Recipe Soup Mix
1/2 cup olive or vegetable oil
1/4 cup butter or margarine, melted
1 teaspoon thyme leaves (optional)
1 teaspoon marjoram leaves (optional)
1/4 teaspoon pepper
2 pounds all-purpose potatoes, cut into quarters

Preheat oven to 450°.

In shallow baking or roasting pan, thoroughly blend all ingredients except potatoes. Add potatoes and turn to coat thoroughly. Bake, stirring occasionally, 40 minutes or until potatoes are tender and golden brown. Garnish, if desired, with chopped parsley.

Makes about 8 servings

❖ CHEESE 'N GRITS CASSEROLE

1 envelope Lipton Golden Onion or Onion Recipe Soup Mix
2 eggs
4 cups hot cooked grits
1 cup shredded Cheddar cheese (about 4 ounces)
1/4 cup butter or margarine, cut into pieces

Preheat oven to 375°.

Beat golden onion recipe soup mix with eggs; set aside.

In large bowl, combine hot grits, cheese and butter. With wire whip or wooden spoon, beat in egg mixture. Turn into lightly greased 1 1/2-quart casserole, then sprinkle, if desired, with paprika. Bake 1 hour or until golden.

Makes about 8 servings

Crisp Onion-Roasted Potatoes

❖ SAVORY LO MEIN

2 tablespoons oil
1 medium clove garlic, finely chopped
1 small head bok choy, cut into 2-inch pieces
    (about 5 cups)*
1 envelope Lipton Onion or Onion-Mushroom
    Recipe Soup Mix
1 cup water
2 tablespoons sherry
1 teaspoon soy sauce
1/4 teaspoon ground ginger
1/2 pound linguine, cooked and drained

In large skillet, heat oil and cook garlic with bok choy over medium-high heat, stirring constantly, 10 minutes or until bok choy is crisp-tender. Stir in onion recipe soup mix blended with water, sherry, soy sauce and ginger. Bring to a boil, then simmer 5 minutes. Add hot linguine and toss lightly; heat through. Sprinkle, if desired, with toasted sesame seeds.

Makes about 4 servings

*Substitution: Use 5 cups coarsely shredded green cabbage. Decrease 10-minute cook time to 3 minutes.

❖ GOLDEN HARVEST STUFFING

1 envelope Lipton Golden Onion Recipe Soup Mix
1²/₃ cups water
1/3 cup orange juice
1 cup dried apricots, quartered
1/4 cup butter or margarine
2 cups chopped celery
1 cup slivered almonds
1/2 pound bulk pork sausage
1 package (7 ounces) seasoned cube stuffing mix
    (about 3¹/₂ cups)

In medium saucepan, thoroughly blend golden onion recipe soup mix, water and orange juice; add apricots. Bring to a boil, then remove from heat and set aside.

In large skillet, melt butter and cook celery with almonds over medium heat until celery is tender. Add sausage and cook, stirring frequently, until sausage is crumbly. Stir in stuffing mix and soup mixture.

*Makes about 6 cups stuffing,
enough for 6 Cornish hens or 1 (10-pound) turkey*

NOTE: Stuffing can also be baked uncovered in a lightly greased 2-quart casserole at 350° for 30 minutes.

❖ BROCCOLI 'N CHEESE PANCAKES

1 envelope Lipton Vegetable Recipe Soup Mix
1/2 cup plain dry bread crumbs
1 package (10 ounces) frozen chopped broccoli,
    cooked and well drained
1 cup shredded Cheddar cheese (about 4 ounces)
1/4 cup milk
2 eggs, slightly beaten
1/4 cup oil

In medium bowl, combine vegetable recipe soup mix with bread crumbs. Stir in broccoli, cheese, milk and eggs until thoroughly combined. Using about 1/4 cup mixture for each, shape into 3-inch-round patties; flatten slightly.

In large skillet, heat oil and cook patties over medium heat, turning once, 3 minutes or until golden brown. Serve warm.

Makes about 12 pancakes

❖ ONION-CHEDDAR BREAD

2¹/₂ cups all-purpose flour
1 cup whole wheat flour
1 package active dry yeast
1/3 cup warm water (105° to 115°)
1/2 cup orange juice
1/2 cup water
2 tablespoons butter or margarine, cut into small
    pieces
1 envelope Lipton Onion Recipe Soup Mix
1 tablespoon sugar
1 teaspoon salt
1¹/₄ cups shredded Cheddar cheese (about 5 ounces)
    Melted butter or margarine

In medium bowl, combine flours; set aside.

In large bowl, dissolve yeast in warm water. Add orange juice, water, butter, onion recipe soup mix, sugar, salt and 2 cups flour mixture; stir until smooth. Stir in remaining flour mixture until dough is easy to handle and pulls away from sides of bowl.

Turn dough onto lightly floured board, then knead until smooth and elastic, about 10 minutes. Cover and let rise in warm place until doubled, about 1 hour. (Dough is ready if indentation remains when touched.)

Preheat oven to 375°. Punch down dough, then turn onto lightly floured board. Press into a 10×8-inch rectangle; top with 1 cup cheese. Roll, starting at 8-inch side, jelly-roll style; pinch ends to seal. Place seam side down in greased 9×5×3-inch loaf pan. Brush with melted butter, then top with remaining cheese. Bake 45 minutes or until bread sounds hollow when tapped. Remove to wire rack; cool completely. *Makes 1 loaf*

Savory Lo Mein

The sauce is also a terrific glaze for chicken and ham!

❖ GLAZED ACORN SQUASH RINGS

1 envelope Lipton Onion or Onion-Mushroom Recipe Soup Mix
1 jar (12 ounces) orange marmalade
1/2 cup orange juice
1/2 cup sliced almonds
1/4 teaspoon ground nutmeg
2 medium acorn squash (about 1 3/4 pounds each), halved, seeded and cut into 1/2-inch rings

Preheat oven to 350°.

In medium bowl, combine all ingredients except squash.

In 13 × 9-inch baking dish, arrange squash; top with marmalade mixture. Bake uncovered, basting occasionally, 40 minutes or until squash is tender.

Makes about 6 servings

❖ SAUTÉED SPINACH & VEGETABLES

2 tablespoons oil
1 cup fresh or canned sliced mushrooms
1 medium clove garlic, finely chopped
1 envelope Lipton Vegetable Recipe Soup Mix
1/2 cup water
2 teaspoons red wine vinegar
1 teaspoon soy sauce
1 package (10 ounces) fresh spinach leaves, washed and drained*

In large skillet, heat oil and cook mushrooms with garlic over medium heat 3 minutes. Stir in vegetable recipe soup mix blended with water, vinegar and soy sauce. Add spinach and toss lightly. Cook over medium heat, stirring constantly, 2 minutes or until spinach is tender.

Makes about 4 servings

*Substitution: Use 1 package (10 ounces) frozen chopped spinach, cooked and drained.

MICROWAVE DIRECTIONS: Decrease oil to 1 tablespoon. In 1-quart casserole, heat spinach, uncovered, at HIGH (Full Power) 4 minutes or until tender. Remove spinach and drain. Add oil and garlic to casserole and heat 1 minute. Stir in vegetable recipe soup mix blended with water, vinegar and soy sauce. Add spinach and mushrooms; toss lightly. Heat covered 3 minutes or until heated through. Let stand covered 5 minutes.

❖ CREAMY BAKED MASHED POTATOES

1 envelope Lipton Vegetable Recipe Soup Mix
4 cups hot mashed potatoes*
1 cup shredded Cheddar or Swiss cheese (about 4 ounces)
1/2 cup chopped green onions (optional)
1 egg, slightly beaten
1/8 teaspoon pepper

Preheat oven to 375°.

In lightly greased 1 1/2-quart casserole, thoroughly combine all ingredients except 1/4 cup cheese. Bake 40 minutes. Top with remaining cheese and bake an additional 5 minutes or until cheese is melted.

Makes about 8 servings

*Do not use salt when preparing hot mashed potatoes.

MICROWAVE DIRECTIONS: In lightly greased 1 1/2-quart casserole, thoroughly combine all ingredients except 1/4 cup cheese. Heat covered at HIGH (Full Power), turning casserole occasionally, 7 minutes or until heated through. Top with remaining cheese, then let stand covered 5 minutes.

❖ VEGETABLE MEDLEY STIR FRY

3 tablespoons oil
Assorted Fresh Vegetables*
1 envelope Lipton Golden Onion Recipe Soup Mix
1 cup water
1/4 teaspoon thyme or basil leaves (optional)
1/8 teaspoon pepper

In large skillet, heat oil and cook Assorted Fresh Vegetables over medium-high heat, stirring frequently, 10 minutes. Stir in golden onion recipe soup mix thoroughly blended with water, thyme and pepper. Bring to a boil, then simmer 12 minutes or until vegetables are crisp-tender. *Makes about 6 servings*

*Assorted Fresh Vegetables: Use any combination of the following to equal 8 cups—broccoli florets, cauliflowerets, sliced red or green peppers, carrots and snow peas.

MICROWAVE DIRECTIONS: Omit oil and decrease water to 2/3 cup. In 2-quart casserole, combine Assorted Fresh Vegetables and golden onion recipe soup mix thoroughly blended with water, thyme and pepper. Heat covered at HIGH (Full Power), stirring occasionally, 11 minutes or until vegetables are crisp-tender.

Creamy Baked Mashed Potatoes

❖ CABBAGE AND APPLE SAUTÉ

2 tablespoons oil
4 cups shredded red or green cabbage (about ½ medium head)
1 medium apple, coarsely chopped
1 envelope Lipton Golden Onion Recipe Soup Mix
1 to 2 teaspoons caraway seeds
⅛ teaspoon pepper
1 cup apple juice

In large skillet, heat oil and cook cabbage with apple over medium heat, stirring occasionally, 5 minutes or until almost tender. Thoroughly blend golden onion recipe soup mix, caraway, pepper and apple juice; stir into cabbage mixture. Simmer uncovered 10 minutes or until cabbage is tender.   *Makes about 4 servings*

MICROWAVE DIRECTIONS: Omit oil. In 2-quart casserole, thoroughly blend golden onion recipe soup mix, caraway, pepper and apple juice. Stir in cabbage and apples and heat uncovered at HIGH (Full Power) 8 minutes, stirring once. Let stand covered 5 minutes.

❖ VEGETABLE RICE PATTIES

1 envelope Lipton Vegetable Recipe Soup Mix
2 cups cooked rice
⅔ cup ricotta or creamed cottage cheese
½ cup shredded mozzarella cheese (about 1½ ounces)
2 eggs, slightly beaten
1 tablespoon grated Parmesan cheese
⅛ teaspoon pepper
½ cup plain dry bread crumbs
   Oil

In large bowl, thoroughly combine vegetable recipe soup mix, rice, ricotta, mozzarella cheese, eggs, Parmesan cheese and pepper. Using about ¼ cup mixture for each, shape into 3-inch-round patties. Coat patties with bread crumbs.

In large skillet, heat ½ inch oil and cook patties over medium heat, turning once, 5 minutes or until golden brown; drain on paper towels. Serve warm.
Makes about 10 patties

MAKE-AHEAD DIRECTIONS: Patties can be partially prepared up to 2 days ahead. Simply shape and coat patties as above. Cover and refrigerate. To serve, heat oil and cook as above.

❖ SWEET POTATO BAKE

2 cans (16 ounces each) sweet potatoes or yams, drained*
1 envelope Lipton Golden Onion Recipe Soup Mix
2 eggs, slightly beaten
½ cup chopped pecans or walnuts
¼ cup butter or margarine, melted
¼ cup brown sugar
½ teaspoon ground cinnamon
⅛ teaspoon ground nutmeg

Preheat oven to 350°.

In large bowl, mash potatoes. Add remaining ingredients and blend thoroughly. Turn into lightly greased 1½-quart casserole, then top, if desired, with flaked coconut. Bake uncovered 30 minutes or until heated through.   *Makes about 8 servings*

*Substitution: Use 4 sweet potatoes or yams (about 2 pounds), cooked and peeled.

❖ BROCCOLI AU GRATIN

1 cup water
1 envelope Lipton Onion-Mushroom or Beefy Mushroom Recipe Soup Mix
3 tablespoons all-purpose flour
1 cup (½ pint) light cream or half and half
1 teaspoon Worcestershire sauce
1 cup shredded Cheddar cheese (about 4 ounces)
1 medium bunch broccoli or 1 medium head cauliflower, separated into large florets and cooked*
Buttered bread crumbs

Preheat oven to 375°.

In medium saucepan, bring water to a boil; stir in onion-mushroom recipe soup mix and simmer covered 5 minutes. Stir in flour blended with cream and Worcestershire sauce. Bring just to the boiling point, then simmer, stirring constantly, until sauce is thickened, about 5 minutes. Stir in cheese until melted.

In 2-quart casserole, arrange broccoli; top with cheese sauce, then bread crumbs. Bake 15 minutes or until heated through.   *Makes about 6 servings*

*Substitution: Use 2 packages (10 ounces each) frozen broccoli spears or cauliflower, cooked and drained.

MICROWAVE DIRECTIONS: In 1½-quart casserole, heat water at HIGH (Full Power) 5 minutes. Stir in onion-mushroom recipe soup mix and heat covered 3 minutes. Stir in flour blended with cream and Worcestershire sauce. Heat uncovered 3 minutes or until sauce is thickened, stirring once. Stir in cheese until melted. Add broccoli, then top with bread crumbs. Heat covered 2 minutes or until heated through. Let stand covered 5 minutes.

Cabbage and Apple Sauté

THE MAIN EVENT

❖ CHICKEN BREASTS FLORENTINE

2 pounds boneless chicken breasts
1/4 cup all-purpose flour
2 eggs, well beaten
2/3 cup seasoned dry bread crumbs
1/4 cup oil
1 medium clove garlic, finely chopped
1/2 cup dry white wine
1 envelope Lipton Golden Onion Recipe Soup Mix
1 1/2 cups water
2 tablespoons finely chopped parsley
1/8 teaspoon pepper
    Hot cooked rice pilaf or white rice
    Hot cooked spinach

Dip chicken in flour, then eggs, then bread crumbs.

In large skillet, heat oil and cook chicken over medium heat until almost done. Remove chicken. Reserve 1 tablespoon drippings. Add garlic and wine to reserved drippings and cook over medium heat 5 minutes. Stir in golden onion recipe soup mix thoroughly blended with water; bring to a boil. Return chicken to skillet and simmer covered 10 minutes or until chicken is done and sauce is slightly thickened. Stir in parsley and pepper. To serve, arrange chicken over hot rice and spinach; garnish as desired.   *Makes about 6 servings*

MICROWAVE DIRECTIONS: Omit oil and decrease wine to 1/4 cup. Dip chicken in flour, eggs and bread crumbs as above. In 3-quart casserole, heat chicken, uncovered, at HIGH (Full Power) 4 minutes, rearranging chicken once. Stir in garlic, then golden onion recipe soup mix thoroughly blended with water and wine. Heat uncovered 5 minutes or until boiling, stirring once. Decrease heat to MEDIUM (50% Full Power) and heat uncovered, stirring occasionally, 7 minutes or until chicken is done and sauce is slightly thickened. Stir in parsley and pepper. Let stand covered 5 minutes. Serve as above.

❖ COUNTRY FRENCH BEEF STEW

2 pounds boneless beef, cut into 1-inch cubes
1/4 cup all-purpose flour
2 slices bacon, cut into 1-inch pieces
3 tablespoons oil
1/4 cup Cognac (optional)
1 envelope Lipton Onion, Beefy Onion, Onion-Mushroom or Beefy Mushroom Recipe Soup Mix
2 cups water
1/2 cup dry red wine
2 tablespoons Dijon-style prepared mustard
3 carrots, thinly sliced
1/2 pound mushrooms, halved
1 package (8 ounces) broad egg noodles

Lightly toss beef with flour; set aside.

In Dutch oven, cook bacon until crisp; remove. Reserve drippings. Heat oil with reserved drippings and brown beef, in three batches, over medium-high heat; remove beef and set aside. Into Dutch oven, add Cognac and cook 1 minute or until only a thin glaze of liquid remains. Stir in onion recipe soup mix blended with water, wine and mustard; bring to a boil. Add beef and bacon and simmer covered, stirring occasionally, 1 1/2 hours or until beef is almost tender. Stir in carrots and simmer covered 25 minutes. Add mushrooms and simmer covered an additional 5 minutes or until beef and vegetables are tender.

Meanwhile, cook noodles according to package directions. To serve, arrange stew over noodles. Garnish, if desired, with chopped parsley.

Makes about 8 servings

Chicken Breasts Florentine

✤ TEX-MEX BAKE

2 cups crushed corn chips
1 egg, beaten
2 tablespoons water
1 envelope Lipton Onion Recipe Soup Mix
1 pound lean ground beef
1 can (4 ounces) chopped green chilies, drained
1 cup shredded Monterey Jack cheese (about 3 ounces)
1 can (8 ounces) tomato sauce
1 medium green pepper, chopped

Preheat oven to 350°.

Combine corn chips, egg and water; press into 9-inch pie plate or casserole. Bake 10 minutes.

Meanwhile, in large bowl, combine onion recipe soup mix, ground beef, chilies and 1/2 cup cheese; evenly press into prepared crust. Top with tomato sauce, then green pepper and bake 30 minutes. Top with remaining cheese, then bake an additional 5 minutes or until cheese is melted and beef is done.

Makes about 6 servings

✤ CHICKEN CURRY

2 tablespoons butter or margarine
1 pound boneless chicken breasts, cut into thin strips
1 large tomato, coarsely chopped
1 envelope Lipton Onion Recipe Soup Mix
2 teaspoons curry powder
1 cup water
1/2 cup plain yogurt
2 cups hot cooked rice
2 cups hot cooked peas

In large skillet, melt butter and brown chicken over medium heat. Stir in tomato, then onion recipe soup mix and curry blended with water. Simmer covered 15 minutes or until chicken is done. Stir in yogurt; heat through, but do not boil. To serve, arrange chicken and sauce over hot rice and peas. Serve, if desired, with flaked coconut, raisins, cashews or almonds.

Makes about 4 servings

MICROWAVE DIRECTIONS: In 2-quart casserole, heat butter at HIGH (Full Power) 1 minute. Add chicken and heat covered 5 minutes. Stir in tomato, then onion recipe soup mix and curry blended with water. Heat covered 6 minutes or until chicken is done. Stir in yogurt; heat 1 minute. Let stand covered 5 minutes. Serve as above.

✤ OLD-FASHIONED POT ROAST

3- to 3½-pound boneless pot roast (rump, chuck or round)
1 envelope Lipton Onion, Beefy Onion, Beefy Mushroom or Onion-Mushroom Recipe Soup Mix
2¼ cups water

In Dutch oven, brown roast over medium heat. Add onion recipe soup mix blended with water. Simmer covered, turning occasionally, 2½ hours or until tender. If desired, thicken gravy. *Makes about 6 servings*

Try some of these delicious international variations!

• **FRENCH-STYLE POT ROAST:** Decrease water to 1¼ cups. Add 1 cup dry red wine and 1 teaspoon thyme leaves.

• **GERMAN-STYLE POT ROAST:** Decrease water to ¾ cup. Add 1½ cups beer, 1 teaspoon brown sugar and ½ teaspoon caraway seeds.

• **ITALIAN-STYLE POT ROAST:** Decrease water to 1 cup. Add 1 can (14½ ounces) whole peeled tomatoes, undrained and chopped, 1 teaspoon basil leaves and 1 bay leaf. (Remove bay leaf before serving.)

MICROWAVE DIRECTIONS: Decrease water to 1¼ cups. In 3-quart casserole, blend onion recipe soup mix with water and heat at HIGH (Full Power) 5 minutes. Add roast and heat uncovered 10 minutes, turning once. Heat covered at DEFROST (30% Full Power), turning occasionally, 50 minutes or until tender. Let stand covered 10 minutes.

✤ ONION-BAKED PORK CHOPS

1 envelope Lipton Golden Onion or Onion Recipe Soup Mix
2/3 cup plain dry bread crumbs
8 pork chops, 1/2 inch thick
2 eggs, well beaten

Preheat oven to 350°.

Combine golden onion recipe soup mix with bread crumbs. Dip chops in eggs, then bread crumb mixture, coating well. In lightly greased large shallow baking pan, arrange chops, then drizzle, if desired, with melted butter. Bake, turning once, 1 hour or until done.

Makes 8 servings

MICROWAVE DIRECTIONS: Dip chops in eggs and bread crumb mixture as above. In lightly greased 3-quart oblong baking dish, heat chops, uncovered, at MEDIUM (50% Full Power) 40 minutes or until chops are done, rearranging chops once. Let stand covered 10 minutes.

Tex-Mex Bake

❖ PORK STEAKS WITH PEPPERS

2 tablespoons olive or vegetable oil
1½ pounds pork blade steaks, ½ inch thick (about 4 to 5)
3 medium red, green or yellow peppers, cut into thin strips
1 clove garlic, finely chopped
1 medium tomato, coarsely chopped
1 envelope Lipton Onion, Onion-Mushroom or Beefy Mushroom Recipe Soup Mix
1 cup water
½ teaspoon thyme leaves
⅛ teaspoon pepper

In large skillet, heat oil and brown steaks over medium-high heat. Remove steaks. Reduce heat to medium; into skillet, add peppers and garlic and cook 5 minutes or until peppers are crisp-tender. Stir in tomato, then onion recipe soup mix blended with water, thyme and pepper; bring to a boil. Return steaks to skillet and simmer uncovered, stirring sauce occasionally, 25 minutes or until steaks and vegetables are tender.

Makes about 4 servings

❖ DELECTABLE BEEF STROGANOFF

2 tablespoons butter or margarine
2 pounds boneless round, chuck or flank steak, cut into thin strips
½ pound mushrooms, sliced
1 envelope Lipton Onion or Beefy Onion Recipe Soup Mix
2¼ cups water
3 tablespoons all-purpose flour
½ cup sour cream

In large skillet, melt butter and brown beef with mushrooms over medium heat. Add onion recipe soup mix blended with 1¾ cups water. Simmer covered, stirring occasionally, 40 minutes or until beef is tender. Stir in flour blended with sour cream and remaining water. Bring just to the boiling point, then simmer, stirring constantly, until sauce is thickened, about 5 minutes. Serve, if desired, over hot cooked noodles.

Makes about 8 servings

MICROWAVE DIRECTIONS: Omit butter. In 3-quart casserole, heat beef, uncovered, at HIGH (Full Power) 5 minutes, stirring once. Add onion recipe soup mix blended with 1¾ cups water and heat covered at DEFROST (30% Full Power), stirring occasionally, 50 minutes or until beef is tender. Add mushrooms and heat covered at DEFROST 5 minutes. Stir in flour blended with sour cream and remaining water. Heat uncovered at DEFROST, stirring occasionally, 10 minutes or until sauce is thickened. Let stand covered 5 minutes. Serve as above.

❖ CHICKEN IN A SKILLET

2 tablespoons oil
2½- to 3-pound chicken, cut into serving pieces
1 can (14½ ounces) whole peeled tomatoes, undrained and chopped
1 envelope Lipton Onion Recipe Soup Mix
⅓ cup water

In large skillet, heat oil and brown chicken over medium-high heat; drain. Add tomatoes, then onion recipe soup mix blended with water. Simmer covered, stirring occasionally, 45 minutes or until chicken is done.

Makes about 4 servings

MICROWAVE DIRECTIONS: Omit oil. In 3-quart casserole, heat chicken, uncovered, at HIGH (Full Power) 12 minutes, rearranging chicken once; drain. Add tomatoes, then onion recipe soup mix blended with water. Heat covered 14 minutes or until chicken is done, rearranging chicken once. Let stand covered 5 minutes.

❖ SOUPER QUICK "LASAGNA"

1½ pounds ground beef
1 envelope Lipton Onion or Onion-Mushroom Recipe Soup Mix
3 cans (8 ounces each) tomato sauce
1 cup water
½ teaspoon oregano (optional)
1 package (8 ounces) broad egg noodles, cooked and drained
1 package (16 ounces) mozzarella cheese, shredded

Preheat oven to 375°.

In large skillet, brown ground beef over medium-high heat; drain. Stir in onion recipe soup mix, tomato sauce, water and oregano. Simmer covered, stirring occasionally, 15 minutes.

In 2-quart oblong baking dish, spoon enough sauce to cover bottom. Alternately layer noodles, ground beef mixture and cheese, ending with cheese. Bake 30 minutes or until bubbling.

Makes about 6 servings

MICROWAVE DIRECTIONS: In 2-quart casserole, heat ground beef, uncovered, at HIGH (Full Power) 7 minutes, stirring once; drain. Stir in onion recipe soup mix, tomato sauce, water and oregano. Heat at MEDIUM (50% Full Power) 5 minutes, stirring once. In 2-quart oblong baking dish, spoon enough sauce to cover bottom. Alternately layer as above. Heat covered at MEDIUM, turning dish occasionally, 10 minutes or until bubbling. Let stand covered 5 minutes.

Pork Steaks with Peppers

✦ FILLETS OF SOLE WITH GARDEN VEGETABLES

2 tablespoons olive or vegetable oil
1 envelope Lipton Golden Onion Recipe Soup Mix
1¾ cups water
¼ cup dry white wine
1 tablespoon lemon juice
2 cups shredded cabbage
2 cups shredded carrots
¼ teaspoon oregano
⅛ teaspoon pepper
1 pound sole or flounder fillets

In large skillet, heat oil and stir in golden onion recipe soup mix thoroughly blended with water, wine and lemon juice. Add cabbage, carrots, oregano and pepper. Cook over medium-high heat, stirring occasionally, 10 minutes or until vegetables are crisp-tender. Remove vegetables to serving platter and keep warm; reserve liquid. Into reserved liquid, add fish and cook 7 minutes or until fish flakes. To serve, arrange fish over vegetables and garnish, if desired, with parsley and lemon slices.   *Makes about 4 servings*

MICROWAVE DIRECTIONS: Omit oil and decrease water to 1½ cups. In 1½-quart casserole, thoroughly blend golden onion recipe soup mix with water, wine and lemon juice. Add cabbage, carrots, oregano and pepper. Heat covered at HIGH (Full Power), stirring occasionally, 8 minutes or until vegetables are crisp-tender. Remove vegetables to serving platter and keep warm; reserve liquid. Into reserved liquid, add fish and heat uncovered 5 minutes or until fish flakes, turning casserole once. Serve and garnish as above.

✦ SLOPPY JOES

2 pounds ground beef
1 envelope Lipton Onion, Onion-Mushroom, Beefy Mushroom or Beefy Onion Recipe Soup Mix
1 can (15 ounces) tomato sauce
½ cup sweet pickle relish

In large skillet, brown ground beef over medium-high heat; drain. Stir in remaining ingredients. Simmer, stirring occasionally, 10 minutes. Serve, if desired, over toasted hamburger rolls.   *Makes about 8 servings*

MICROWAVE DIRECTIONS: In 2-quart casserole, heat ground beef, uncovered, at HIGH (Full Power) 7 minutes; drain. Stir in remaining ingredients. Heat covered, stirring occasionally, 4 minutes or until heated through. Let stand covered 5 minutes. Serve as above.

Fillets of Sole with Garden Vegetables

✦ BEEF & VEGETABLE SKILLET DINNER

2 tablespoons oil
1 pound boneless sirloin steak, cut into thin strips
1 cup frozen sliced carrots
1 envelope Lipton Beefy Mushroom, Onion or Onion-Mushroom Recipe Soup Mix
1 cup water
2 tablespoons soy sauce
2 tablespoons ketchup
½ teaspoon garlic powder
¼ teaspoon ground ginger
1 can (8 ounces) bamboo shoots, drained
1 package (6 ounces) frozen snow peas, thawed
Hot cooked rice

In large skillet, heat oil and brown beef, in two batches, over medium-high heat. Remove beef. Add carrots, then beefy mushroom recipe soup mix blended with water, soy sauce, ketchup, garlic powder and ginger. Bring to a boil, then simmer, stirring occasionally, 5 minutes or until carrots are crisp-tender. Add beef, bamboo shoots and snow peas; simmer 3 minutes or until heated through. To serve, arrange beef mixture over hot rice.   *Makes about 4 servings*

✦ RAISIN-STUFFED CORNISH GAME HENS WITH APPLES

1 envelope Lipton Onion Recipe Soup Mix
1¼ cups apple cider or juice
2 cups unseasoned cube stuffing mix
⅓ cup raisins
⅓ cup coarsely chopped walnuts
4 Cornish hens (1 to 1½ pounds each)
2 large apples, cored and halved
¼ cup brown sugar
½ teaspoon ground cinnamon

Preheat oven to 375°.

In medium bowl, blend onion recipe soup mix with cider. Pour ½ mixture into medium bowl; stir in stuffing mix, raisins and walnuts. Stuff hens with raisin mixture; secure cavities with poultry pins or skewers. In shallow baking pan, arrange hens and apples.

To remaining cider mixture, blend in sugar and cinnamon; brush hens and apples with ½ mixture. Bake, brushing occasionally with remaining glaze mixture, 1 hour or until hens are done. To serve, on large serving platter, arrange hens and apples, sliced.
        Makes 4 servings

MICROWAVE DIRECTIONS: Prepare hens and glaze mixture as above. Slice apples in quarters. In 3-quart oblong baking dish, arrange hens and apples; brush with ½ glaze. Heat at HIGH (Full Power), brushing occasionally with remaining glaze and turning dish occasionally, 45 minutes or until hens are done. Let stand covered 5 minutes. Serve as above.

❖ CHICKEN ROMA

2 tablespoons oil
2½- to 3-pound chicken, cut into serving pieces
1 can (14½ ounces) whole peeled tomatoes,
    undrained and chopped
½ cup sliced pitted ripe olives
1 clove garlic, finely chopped
1 envelope Lipton Onion, Onion-Mushroom, Beefy
    Mushroom or Beefy Onion Recipe Soup Mix
¼ cup dry red wine
1 package (8 ounces) broad egg noodles

In large skillet, heat oil and brown chicken over medium-high heat; drain. Add tomatoes, olives and garlic, then onion recipe soup mix blended with wine. Simmer covered 40 minutes or until chicken is done.

Meanwhile, cook noodles according to package directions. If necessary, skim fat from sauce. To serve, arrange chicken and sauce over hot noodles.

Makes about 4 servings

MICROWAVE DIRECTIONS: Omit oil. In 2-quart casserole, heat chicken at HIGH (Full Power) 12 minutes, rearranging chicken once; drain. Add tomatoes, olives and garlic, then onion recipe soup mix blended with wine. Heat covered 14 minutes or until chicken is done, rearranging chicken once. Let stand covered 5 minutes. Serve as above.

❖ FAST 'N EASY CHILI

1½ pounds ground beef
1½ cups water
1 can (8 ounces) tomato sauce
1 envelope Lipton Onion, Onion-Mushroom, Beefy
    Mushroom or Beefy Onion Recipe Soup Mix
1 tablespoon chili powder*
1 can (16 ounces) red kidney beans, drained

In large skillet, brown ground beef over medium-high heat; drain. Stir in remaining ingredients. Simmer covered, stirring occasionally, 20 minutes.

Makes about 6 servings

*Variations—

● **FIRST ALARM CHILI:** Add 4 teaspoons chili powder.

● **SECOND ALARM CHILI:** Add 2 tablespoons chili powder.

● **THIRD ALARM CHILI:** Add chili powder at your own risk.

MICROWAVE DIRECTIONS: In 2-quart casserole, heat ground beef at HIGH (Full Power) 4 minutes; drain. Stir in remaining ingredients. Heat covered, stirring occasionally, 10 minutes or until heated through. Let stand covered 5 minutes.

❖ PHYLLO SPINACH PIE

1 container (15 ounces) ricotta cheese
1 package (10 ounces) frozen chopped spinach,
    cooked and squeezed dry
2 eggs, slightly beaten
2 tablespoons grated Parmesan cheese
1 envelope Lipton Vegetable Recipe Soup Mix
¼ teaspoon ground nutmeg
2 cups fresh or canned sliced mushrooms
15 phyllo strudel sheets
½ cup butter or margarine, melted

Preheat oven to 375°.

In large bowl, thoroughly combine ricotta, spinach, eggs, Parmesan cheese, vegetable recipe soup mix and nutmeg; stir in mushrooms and set aside.

Unfold phyllo strudel sheets; cover with wax paper, then damp cloth. Brush 1 sheet at a time with melted butter. Place 6 buttered sheets across 9-inch pie plate, extending sheets over sides; press gently into pie plate (see illustration). Place an additional 6 buttered sheets in opposite direction across 9-inch pie plate, extending sheets over sides, to form a cross; press gently into pie plate. Turn spinach mixture into prepared pie plate; gently fold sheets over spinach mixture to cover. Form remaining 3 buttered sheets into a ball and place on center of pie; brush with butter. Bake 35 minutes or until golden. Let stand 10 minutes before serving.

Makes about 8 servings

FREEZING DIRECTIONS: Pie can be frozen up to 1 month. Simply prepare as above, but do not brush with butter or bake. Wrap in heavy-duty aluminum foil; freeze. To serve, unwrap, then brush with butter as above and bake at 375°, 40 minutes or until golden. Let stand as above.

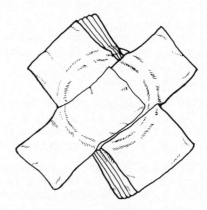

Phyllo Spinach Pie

Fettuccine with Shrimp and Creamy Herb Sauce

❖ FETTUCCINE WITH SHRIMP AND CREAMY HERB SAUCE

  1 envelope Lipton Creamy Herb Recipe Soup Mix
1³/4 cups milk
  8 ounces frozen cleaned shrimp, partially thawed*
¹/2 cup frozen peas, partially thawed
  6 ounces fettuccine or medium egg noodles, cooked and drained
¹/4 cup grated Parmesan cheese

In 2-quart saucepan, with wire whip or fork, thoroughly blend creamy herb recipe soup mix with milk. Bring just to the boiling point, stirring frequently. Add shrimp and peas and simmer 3 minutes or until shrimp are tender. Toss shrimp sauce with hot noodles and cheese.

Makes about 2 servings

*Substitution: Use 8 ounces uncooked fresh shrimp, cleaned.

MICROWAVE DIRECTIONS: Decrease milk to 1¹/4 cups. In 2-quart casserole, with wire whip or fork, thoroughly blend creamy herb recipe soup mix with milk. Heat uncovered at HIGH (Full Power), stirring occasionally, 5 minutes. Add shrimp and peas and heat uncovered, stirring occasionally, 6 minutes or until shrimp are tender. Toss as above.

❖ STEAK WITH SAVORY HERB SAUCE

  1 envelope Lipton Creamy Herb Recipe Soup Mix
1¹/4 cups water
  1 tablespoon red wine vinegar
  Freshly ground pepper to taste
  4 tenderloin, sirloin or minute steaks (4 ounces each)
  3 cups hot cooked rice
  1 cup sliced mushrooms, cooked

In 1-quart saucepan, with wire whip or fork, thoroughly blend creamy herb recipe soup mix, water and vinegar. Bring to a boil, stirring frequently, then reduce heat and simmer, stirring occasionally, 5 minutes; add pepper.

Meanwhile, broil or pan-fry steaks until tender; keep warm. To serve, arrange steaks over hot rice combined with mushrooms, then top with sauce.

Makes about 4 servings

MICROWAVE DIRECTIONS: Increase water to 1¹/3 cups. In 1-quart casserole, with wire whip or fork, thoroughly blend creamy herb recipe soup mix, water and vinegar. Heat uncovered at HIGH (Full Power), stirring occasionally, 5 minutes; add pepper. Prepare steaks and serve as above.

❖ SOUPERIOR MEAT LOAF

1 envelope Lipton Beefy Onion, Onion, Onion-
   Mushroom or Beefy Mushroom Recipe Soup
   Mix
2 pounds ground beef
1½ cups fresh bread crumbs
2 eggs
¾ cup water
⅓ cup ketchup

Preheat oven to 350°.

In large bowl, combine all ingredients. In large shallow
baking pan, shape into loaf. Bake 1 hour or until done.
Makes about 8 servings

MICROWAVE DIRECTIONS: Combine as above. In 2-
quart oblong baking dish, shape into loaf. Heat
uncovered at HIGH (Full Power), turning dish
occasionally, 25 minutes or until done; drain. Let stand
covered 5 minutes.

❖ OLD-FASHIONED CHICKEN POT PIE

3 tablespoons butter or margarine
3 tablespoons all-purpose flour
¼ cup chopped green onion
1 envelope Lipton Vegetable Recipe Soup Mix
2 cups milk
2 cups cut-up cooked chicken
1 package (10 ounces) frozen broccoli spears,
   cooked, drained and cut into 1-inch pieces
¼ cup grated Parmesan cheese
⅛ teaspoon pepper
   Pastry for single-crust pie
1 egg yolk
2 tablespoons water

Preheat oven to 425°.

In large saucepan, melt butter and cook flour with
green onion over medium heat, stirring constantly, 3
minutes or until flour is bubbling. Stir in vegetable
recipe soup mix blended with milk. Bring just to the
boiling point, then simmer, stirring constantly, 5
minutes or until thickened. Stir in chicken, broccoli,
cheese and pepper. Turn into lightly greased 1-quart
round casserole or soufflé dish.

With rolling pin, roll pastry into a 9-inch circle; arrange
over casserole. Press pastry around edge of casserole to
seal; trim excess pastry, then flute edges. Brush pastry
with egg yolk beaten with water. With tip of knife,
make small slits in pastry. Bake 40 minutes or until
crust is golden. *Makes about 4 servings*

❖ APRICOT-STUFFED LAMB CHOPS

4 double loin lamb chops, 2 inches thick (about 2
   pounds)
4 dried apricots, halved
1 envelope Lipton Onion or Onion-Mushroom
   Recipe Soup Mix
1 cup water
¼ cup olive or vegetable oil
¼ cup honey
2 tablespoons Dijon-style prepared mustard
2 teaspoons rosemary leaves
½ teaspoon ground ginger

With knife parallel to cutting board, make a 1-inch-wide
by 1-inch-deep cut in meaty side of each chop. Stuff
each cut with 2 apricot halves; press firmly to close.

In shallow glass baking dish, combine remaining
ingredients; add chops and turn to coat. Cover and
marinate in refrigerator, turning occasionally, at least 2
hours.

Preheat oven to 425°. Bake chops with marinade,
basting and turning chops occasionally, 35 minutes or
until meat thermometer reaches 145° (rare), 155°
(medium) or 165° (well done).
Makes about 4 servings

❖ SHRIMPLY DELICIOUS CREOLE

2 tablespoons butter or margarine
¾ cup chopped green pepper
½ cup chopped celery
1 can (14½ ounces) whole peeled tomatoes,
   undrained and chopped
1 tablespoon finely chopped parsley
1 envelope Lipton Golden Onion Recipe Soup Mix
½ cup water
1 pound uncooked shrimp, cleaned

In large skillet, melt butter and cook green pepper with
celery over medium heat until tender. Add tomatoes
and parsley, then golden onion recipe soup mix
blended with water. Bring to a boil, then simmer
covered, stirring occasionally, 20 minutes. Add shrimp
and cook 5 minutes or until shrimp are done. Serve, if
desired, over hot cooked rice.
Makes about 4 servings

MICROWAVE DIRECTIONS: In 1½-quart casserole,
heat butter, green pepper and celery at HIGH (Full
Power) 5 minutes, stirring once. Stir in tomatoes and
parsley, then golden onion recipe soup mix blended
with water. Heat covered 5 minutes, stirring once. Add
shrimp and heat covered 5 minutes or until shrimp are
done. Let stand covered 5 minutes. Serve as above.

❖ CHICKEN 'N VEGETABLE STIR FRY

3 tablespoons oil
1 pound boneless chicken breasts, cut into thin strips
1/2 cup broccoli florets
2 ounces snow peas (about 1/2 cup)
1 medium carrot, thinly sliced
1/2 medium red or green pepper, cut into thin strips
1 envelope Lipton Golden Onion Recipe Soup Mix
1 teaspoon cornstarch
1/2 teaspoon ground ginger
1 1/2 cups water
2 teaspoons soy sauce
1 teaspoon white or rice vinegar
Hot cooked rice

In large skillet, heat oil and cook chicken with vegetables over medium-high heat, stirring constantly, 10 minutes or until chicken is golden and vegetables are crisp-tender. Thoroughly blend golden onion recipe soup mix, cornstarch, ginger, water, soy sauce and vinegar; stir into chicken mixture. Bring to a boil, then simmer uncovered 5 minutes or until sauce is thickened. Serve over hot rice and garnish, if desired, with sliced green onion and toasted sesame seeds.

Makes about 4 servings

MICROWAVE DIRECTIONS: Omit oil and decrease ginger to 1/4 teaspoon. In 2-quart casserole, heat chicken, uncovered, at HIGH (Full Power) 4 minutes or until almost done; remove chicken and drain. Add vegetables to casserole and heat uncovered 5 minutes. Thoroughly blend golden onion recipe soup mix, cornstarch, ginger, water, soy sauce and vinegar; stir into vegetables. Heat uncovered 5 minutes or until sauce is thickened, stirring once. Return chicken to casserole and heat 1 minute or until heated through. Let stand covered 5 minutes. Serve and garnish as above.

❖ ALL-IN-ONE TUNA CASSEROLE

1 envelope Lipton Golden Onion Recipe Soup Mix
1 1/2 cups milk
1 package (10 ounces) frozen peas and carrots, thawed
1 package (8 ounces) medium egg noodles, cooked and drained
1 can (6 1/2 ounces) tuna, drained and flaked
1/2 cup shredded Cheddar cheese (about 2 ounces)

Preheat oven to 350°.

In large bowl, blend golden onion recipe soup mix with milk; stir in peas and carrots, cooked noodles and tuna. Turn into greased 2-quart oblong baking dish, then top with cheese. Bake 20 minutes or until bubbling. *Makes about 4 servings*

❖ OVEN-BAKED BOURGUIGNONNE

2 pounds boneless beef chuck, cut into 1-inch cubes
1/4 cup all-purpose flour
1 1/3 cups sliced carrots
1 can (14 1/2 ounces) whole peeled tomatoes, undrained and chopped
1 bay leaf
1 envelope Lipton Beefy Onion or Onion Recipe Soup Mix
1/2 cup dry red wine
1 cup fresh or canned sliced mushrooms
1 package (8 ounces) medium or broad egg noodles

Preheat oven to 400°.

In 2-quart casserole, toss beef with flour, then bake uncovered 20 minutes. Add carrots, tomatoes and bay leaf, then beefy onion recipe soup mix blended with wine. Bake covered 1 1/2 hours or until beef is tender. Add mushrooms and bake covered an additional 10 minutes. Remove bay leaf.

Meanwhile, cook noodles according to package directions. To serve, arrange bourguignonne over noodles. *Makes about 8 servings*

MICROWAVE DIRECTIONS: Toss beef with flour; set aside. In 2-quart casserole, combine tomatoes, bay leaf and beefy onion recipe soup mix blended with wine. Heat covered at HIGH (Full Power) 7 minutes, stirring once. Add beef and carrots. Heat covered at DEFROST (30% Full Power), stirring occasionally, 1 1/4 hours. Add mushrooms and heat covered at DEFROST 30 minutes or until beef is tender. Remove bay leaf. Let stand covered 5 minutes. Cook noodles and serve as above.

FREEZING/REHEATING DIRECTIONS:
Bourguignonne can be baked, then frozen. Simply wrap covered casserole in heavy-duty aluminum foil; freeze. To reheat, unwrap and bake covered at 400°, stirring occasionally to separate beef and vegetables, 1 hour. **OR,** microwave at HIGH (Full Power), stirring occasionally, 20 minutes or until heated through. Let stand covered 5 minutes.

Chicken 'n Vegetable Stir Fry

❖ BAKED HAM WITH WINE & ONION GLAZE

1 envelope Lipton Onion or Onion-Mushroom
    Recipe Soup Mix
1 cup water
1/3 cup brown sugar
1/4 cup Madeira wine or sherry
2 tablespoons butter or margarine, melted
1 tablespoon finely chopped parsley
5- to 6-pound fully-cooked ham butt end
1 pound shallots or small onions, peeled and
    quartered

Preheat oven to 375°.

In small bowl, blend onion recipe soup mix, water, sugar, wine, butter and parsley; set aside.

In roasting pan, place ham. With knife, score (lightly cut) fat in diamond pattern; top with soup mixture. Arrange shallots around ham. Bake, stirring shallots and basting ham occasionally, 60 minutes or until golden brown.
Makes about 8 servings

❖ BAKED CHICKEN BREASTS WITH RICE & VEGETABLE STUFFING

1 envelope Lipton Vegetable Recipe Soup Mix
1 1/2 cups water
1/2 cup uncooked regular rice
1 package (10 ounces) frozen chopped spinach,
    cooked and squeezed dry
1/2 medium tomato, coarsely chopped
1/2 cup shredded mozzarella cheese (about 1 1/2
    ounces)
1/4 cup grated Parmesan cheese
1 small clove garlic, finely chopped
4 whole boneless chicken breasts (about 2
    pounds), skinned and halved

In medium saucepan, blend vegetable recipe soup mix with water; bring to a boil. Stir in uncooked rice and simmer covered 20 minutes or until tender. Stir in spinach, tomato, cheeses and garlic; set aside.

Preheat oven to 350°. With knife parallel to cutting board, make deep, 3-inch-long cut in center of each chicken breast half to form pocket. Evenly stuff pockets with rice mixture.

In lightly greased baking dish, arrange chicken and bake uncovered, basting occasionally, 40 minutes or until done. Sprinkle, if desired, with paprika.
Makes about 8 servings

❖ PORK ROAST WITH SAUSAGE & SPINACH STUFFING

1 envelope Lipton Onion, Onion-Mushroom or
    Beefy Mushroom Recipe Soup Mix
1 package (10 ounces) frozen chopped spinach,
    cooked and drained
1/2 pound sweet Italian sausage links, removed from
    casing
1/2 cup fresh bread crumbs
1/2 cup slivered almonds, toasted
2 eggs, slightly beaten
2 tablespoons finely chopped parsley
2 teaspoons thyme leaves
1 teaspoon finely chopped garlic (about 1 medium
    clove)
1/8 teaspoon pepper
2 1/2-pound boneless center cut pork loin roast
1 to 2 tablespoons oil

Preheat oven to 350°.

In large bowl, thoroughly combine onion recipe soup mix, spinach, sausage, bread crumbs, almonds, eggs, parsley, 1 teaspoon thyme, 1/2 teaspoon garlic and pepper; set aside.

Butterfly roast as directed. Spread spinach mixture evenly on cut side of roast. Roll, starting at long end, jelly-roll style; tie securely with string. In roasting pan, on rack, place pork seam side down. Rub roast with oil, then top with remaining garlic and thyme. Roast for 1 1/2 hours or until meat thermometer reaches 165° (medium) or 180° (well done).
Makes about 8 servings

HOW TO BUTTERFLY A PORK LOIN ROAST

1. Place the boneless roast fat side down. Starting at the thickest edge, slice horizontally through the meat, stopping 1 inch from the opposite edge so that the roast can open like a book.

2. Lightly pound the opened roast and remove any fat thicker than 1/4 inch.

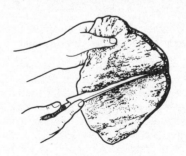

Pork Roast with Sausage & Spinach Stuffing

❖ SCALLOPS WITH GOLDEN CREAM SAUCE

2 tablespoons butter or margarine
1 medium red pepper, cut into thin strips
1 cup uncooked regular rice
1 envelope Lipton Golden Onion Recipe Soup Mix
2¼ cups water
1 tablespoon lime juice
¼ cup light cream or half and half
1 pound bay scallops
2 medium green onions, sliced

In medium skillet, melt butter and cook red pepper over medium heat until crisp-tender. Stir in uncooked rice, then golden onion recipe soup mix thoroughly blended with water and lime juice. Bring to a boil, then simmer covered 30 minutes or until rice is tender. Stir in remaining ingredients and cook covered 5 minutes or until scallops are tender. Serve, if desired, with freshly ground pepper.   *Makes about 4 servings*

❖ POULET A LA JARDINIÈRE

2 whole boneless chicken breasts (about 1½ pounds), halved and lightly pounded
Pepper
2 tablespoons chopped parsley
8 pieces carrot, about 3 × ¼ inch each
2 tablespoons butter or margarine
1 bay leaf
1 envelope Lipton Onion-Mushroom Recipe Soup Mix*
1¼ cups water
¾ cup dry white wine
1 tablespoon cornstarch

Sprinkle each chicken breast half with pepper and ½ tablespoon parsley, then top with 2 carrot pieces; roll up and secure with wooden toothpicks.

In medium skillet, melt butter and brown chicken over medium heat. Add bay leaf, then onion-mushroom recipe soup mix blended with 1 cup water and wine. Simmer covered 15 minutes or until chicken is done. Stir in cornstarch blended with remaining water. Bring to a boil, then simmer, stirring constantly, until sauce is thickened, about 5 minutes. Remove bay leaf.
Makes about 4 servings

*Variation: Use Lipton Beefy Mushroom Recipe Soup Mix and decrease cornstarch to 2 teaspoons.

MICROWAVE DIRECTIONS: Decrease water to ¾ cup. Roll chicken as above. In 2-quart oblong baking dish, heat butter at HIGH (Full Power) 2 minutes. Add chicken and heat covered 5 minutes. Add bay leaf, then onion-mushroom recipe soup mix blended with cornstarch, water and wine. Heat uncovered 8 minutes or until chicken is done, rearranging chicken once. Let stand covered 5 minutes. Remove bay leaf.

❖ BAKED EGGPLANT WITH VEGETABLE-CHEESE STUFFING

1 medium eggplant (about 1½ pounds), peeled
Salt
1 container (15 ounces) ricotta cheese
1½ cups shredded mozzarella cheese (about 6 ounces)
2 eggs, slightly beaten
1 envelope Lipton Vegetable Recipe Soup Mix
2 tablespoons grated Parmesan cheese
2 tablespoons finely chopped parsley
2 cups (16 ounces) spaghetti sauce

Cut eggplant lengthwise into ⅛-inch-thick slices; sprinkle lightly with salt. Let stand at room temperature at least 30 minutes. Drain, then rinse thoroughly; pat dry with paper towels.

Preheat oven to 350°. In medium bowl, thoroughly combine ricotta, 1 cup mozzarella cheese, eggs, vegetable recipe soup mix, Parmesan cheese and parsley. Spoon about ¼ cup cheese mixture onto center of each eggplant slice; roll up and arrange in greased 2-quart oblong baking dish. Top with sauce, then remaining mozzarella cheese. Bake uncovered 40 minutes or until eggplant is tender.
Makes about 4 servings

MAKE-AHEAD DIRECTIONS: Eggplant can be partially prepared up to 1 day ahead. Simply prepare eggplant and roll up as above. Cover and refrigerate. To serve, top with sauce, then remaining mozzarella cheese and bake as above.

❖ SPICY NACHO BAKE

1 pound ground beef
1 can (4 ounces) chopped green chilies, drained
1 envelope Lipton Nacho Cheese Recipe Soup Mix
1 cup water
½ cup sour cream
1 cup coarsely chopped tomato
6 corn tortillas

Preheat oven to 375°.

In medium skillet, brown ground beef over medium-high heat; drain. Stir in chilies, then nacho cheese recipe soup mix thoroughly blended with water. Bring to a boil, then simmer, stirring occasionally, 5 minutes. Stir in sour cream and tomato.

In greased 1½-quart oblong baking dish, alternately layer tortillas and ground beef mixture, ending with beef mixture. Bake 15 minutes or until heated through.
Makes about 4 servings

❖ MINI TORTILLA PIZZAS

2 tablespoons oil
1 medium green pepper, coarsely chopped
1 envelope Lipton Onion or Onion-Mushroom
    Recipe Soup Mix
1 can (8 ounces) tomato sauce
1 cup water
1 teaspoon chili powder
1/2 teaspoon ground cumin (optional)
2 cups cut-up cooked chicken
4 corn or flour tortillas
2 cups shredded Monterey Jack or Cheddar cheese
    (about 8 ounces)

Preheat oven to 375°.

In large saucepan, heat oil and cook green pepper over medium heat until tender. Stir in onion recipe soup mix, tomato sauce, water, chili powder and cumin. Bring to a boil, then simmer, stirring occasionally, 10 minutes. Stir in chicken.

Meanwhile, on baking sheet, arrange tortillas. If desired, lightly brush tortillas with additional oil for extra crispness. Spoon chicken mixture evenly on tortillas, then top with cheese. Bake 15 minutes or until cheese is melted and sauce is bubbling. Serve, if desired, with sour cream, chopped tomato and additional shredded cheese. Garnish, if desired, with jalapeño peppers.

Makes 4 servings

❖ GRILLED FISH STEAKS WITH VEGETABLE BUTTER

1 envelope Lipton Vegetable Recipe Soup Mix
1/2 cup butter or margarine, softened
2 tablespoons brandy or sherry
1/2 teaspoon ground ginger
4 halibut, cod, swordfish, salmon or shark steaks
    (about 2 pounds), 1/2 inch thick
1/2 cup orange juice
1/4 cup oil

In medium bowl, with electric mixer or rotary beater, thoroughly blend vegetable recipe soup mix, butter, brandy and ginger. Turn onto wax paper and shape into 8×2-inch log. Wrap in plastic wrap or wax paper, then chill until firm.

Meanwhile, in large baking dish, arrange fish; add orange juice and oil. Cover and marinate in refrigerator, turning occasionally, at least 1 hour. Remove fish from marinade. Grill or broil until fish flakes. To serve, top each steak with 1/2-inch slice butter mixture.

Makes 4 servings

MICROWAVE DIRECTIONS: Prepare butter mixture and marinate fish as above. In 13×9-inch baking dish, arrange fish and heat uncovered at HIGH (Full Power), rearranging fish occasionally, 9 minutes or until fish flakes. Top with butter as above. Let stand covered 5 minutes.

Mini Tortilla Pizzas

❖ MUSHROOM & PEPPER STUFFED CHOPS

    2 tablespoons butter or margarine
 1/2 pound mushrooms, sliced
    1 small red or green pepper, chopped
 1/2 cup sliced almonds
    1 envelope Lipton Onion or Onion-Mushroom
       Recipe Soup Mix
    1 cup fresh bread crumbs
 1/8 teaspoon pepper
    4 double loin pork or veal chops, 2 inches thick
       (about 2 1/2 pounds)

Preheat oven to 350°.

In medium skillet, heat butter and cook mushrooms, red pepper and almonds over medium-high heat 5 minutes or until vegetables are tender. Remove from heat, then stir in onion recipe soup mix combined with bread crumbs and pepper; set aside.

With knife parallel to cutting board, make a deep cut in meaty side of each chop. Evenly stuff each cut with mushroom mixture; secure, if desired, with skewers.

In shallow baking pan, arrange chops and bake 1 hour or until done.   *Makes about 4 servings*

❖ ROASTED CHICKEN WITH DILL

    1 envelope Lipton Golden Onion or Onion Recipe
       Soup Mix
    1 cup loosely packed snipped fresh dill*
 1/4 cup olive or vegetable oil
    4 large cloves garlic, chopped
 1/4 teaspoon pepper
    5- to 6-pound roasting chicken

Preheat oven to 375°.

In food processor or blender, combine all ingredients except chicken until blended.

In roasting pan, on rack, place chicken; spread dill mixture inside cavity, then under and over skin. Close cavity with poultry pins or wooden toothpicks; tie legs together with string. Cover with heavy-duty aluminum foil, then roast 1 1/2 hours. Remove foil and continue roasting 15 minutes or until meat thermometer reaches 185°.   *Makes about 4 servings*

*Substitution: Use 2 tablespoons dried dill weed.

❖ TURKEY COTTAGE PIE

 1/4 cup butter or margarine
 1/4 cup all-purpose flour
    1 envelope Lipton Golden Onion Recipe Soup Mix
    2 cups water
    2 cups cut-up cooked turkey or chicken
    1 package (10 ounces) frozen mixed vegetables,
       thawed
 1 1/4 cups shredded Swiss cheese (about 5 ounces)
 1/8 teaspoon pepper
    5 cups hot mashed potatoes

Preheat oven to 375°.

In large saucepan, melt butter and cook flour over medium-low heat, stirring constantly, 5 minutes or until golden. Stir in golden onion recipe soup mix thoroughly blended with water. Bring to a boil, then simmer 15 minutes or until thickened. Stir in turkey, vegetables, 1 cup cheese and pepper. Turn into lightly greased 2-quart casserole; top with hot potatoes, then remaining cheese. Bake 30 minutes or until bubbling.
Makes about 8 servings

MICROWAVE DIRECTIONS: In 2-quart casserole, heat butter at HIGH (Full Power) 1 minute. Stir in flour and heat uncovered, stirring frequently, 2 minutes. Stir in golden onion recipe soup mix thoroughly blended with water. Heat uncovered, stirring occasionally, 4 minutes or until thickened. Stir in turkey, vegetables, 1 cup cheese and pepper. Top with hot potatoes, then remaining cheese. Heat uncovered, turning casserole occasionally, 5 minutes or until bubbling. Let stand uncovered 5 minutes. For additional color, sprinkle, if desired, with paprika.

❖ CHICKEN PACIFICA

    2 tablespoons oil
 2 1/2- to 3-pound chicken, cut into serving pieces
    1 can (8 ounces) pineapple chunks in natural juice,
       drained (reserve juice)
       Water
    1 envelope Lipton Onion Recipe Soup Mix
    2 tablespoons all-purpose flour

In large skillet, heat oil and brown chicken over medium-high heat. Mix reserved juice with enough water to equal 2 cups; blend in onion recipe soup mix. Add to skillet and simmer covered, stirring occasionally, 45 minutes or until chicken is done. Remove chicken to serving platter and keep warm. Into skillet, add flour blended with 1/4 cup water. Bring to a boil, then simmer, stirring constantly, until sauce is slightly thickened, about 5 minutes. Add pineapple and heat through. Serve sauce with chicken.
Makes about 4 servings

Turkey Cottage Pie

LET THE GOOD TIMES ROLL

OUTDOOR EXTRAVAGANZA

✦ OVEN-BAKED BUTTERMILK CHICKEN

1 envelope Lipton Golden Onion Recipe Soup Mix
1 cup all-purpose flour
2 eggs
1/2 cup buttermilk*
2 1/2- to 3-pound chicken, cut into serving pieces
1/4 cup butter or margarine, melted

Preheat oven to 425°.

Combine golden onion recipe soup mix with flour; set aside.

Beat eggs with buttermilk. Dip chicken in buttermilk mixture, then flour mixture, coating well. Place in large shallow baking pan, on rack, and chill 30 minutes. Drizzle with butter, then bake 45 minutes or until done.
Makes about 4 servings

*Substitution: Blend 1 1/2 teaspoons lemon juice with enough milk to equal 1/2 cup; let stand 5 minutes.

✦ SWEET 'N SPICY ONION GLAZE

1 envelope Lipton Onion Recipe Soup Mix
1 jar (20 ounces) apricot preserves
1 cup (8 ounces) Wish-Bone® Russian or Sweet 'n Spicy® French Dressing

In small bowl, blend all ingredients. Use as a glaze for chicken, spareribs, kabobs, hamburgers or frankfurters. Brush on during the last half of cooking.
Makes about 2 1/2 cups glaze

✦ SUMMERTIME'S BOUNTY PIE

1 envelope Lipton Onion, Onion-Mushroom, Beefy Mushroom or Beefy Onion Recipe Soup Mix
1 1/2 pounds ground beef
2 cups fresh bread crumbs
1/2 pint (8 ounces) sour cream
1 egg
1/4 teaspoon thyme or basil leaves
1 tablespoon all-purpose flour
1 1/2 cups shredded Cheddar cheese (about 6 ounces)
3 1/2 cups hot cooked assorted vegetables

Preheat oven to 350°.

In large bowl, combine onion recipe soup mix, ground beef, bread crumbs, sour cream, egg and thyme.

Sprinkle flour into 9-inch pie pan. Press ground beef mixture onto bottom and sides of prepared pan, shaping edges 3/4 inch above pan and forming a center "well." Bake 40 minutes; drain. Fill with 3/4 cup cheese, then vegetables and remaining cheese. Bake an additional 10 minutes or until cheese is melted.
Makes about 6 servings

MICROWAVE DIRECTIONS: In 9-inch glass pie plate, prepare ground beef mixture as above. Heat uncovered at HIGH (Full Power) 9 minutes, turning plate every 3 minutes; drain. Fill as above and heat 3 minutes or until cheese is melted. Let stand covered 5 minutes.

Oven-Baked Buttermilk Chicken

✤ SAVORY ONION CHEESE TART

1 envelope Lipton Golden Onion Recipe Soup Mix
1 cup milk
1 egg, slightly beaten
½ teaspoon rosemary leaves
1 package (8 ounces) mozzarella cheese, shredded
1 package (15 ounces) refrigerated pie crusts for 2 (9-inch) crusts

In small bowl, thoroughly blend golden onion recipe soup mix, milk, egg and rosemary. Stir in cheese. Freeze 1 hour or refrigerate at least 2 hours until mixture is slightly thickened and not runny.

Preheat oven to 375°. On two aluminum-foil-lined baking sheets, unfold pie crusts. Fold crust edges over 1 inch to form rim. Brush, if desired, with 1 egg yolk beaten with 2 tablespoons water. Fill center of each prepared crust with ½ soup mixture; spread evenly to rim. Bake 25 minutes or until crusts are golden brown. To serve, cut into wedges. *Makes 2 tarts*

FREEZING/REHEATING DIRECTIONS: Tarts can be baked, then frozen. Simply wrap in heavy-duty aluminum foil; freeze. To reheat, unwrap and bake at 350° until heated through.

✤ CHICKEN MARINATED WITH ORANGE & TARRAGON

1 envelope Lipton Onion or Onion-Mushroom Recipe Soup Mix
1 jar (12 ounces) orange marmalade
1 cup orange juice
1 teaspoon tarragon leaves
2½- to 3-pound chicken, cut into serving pieces
Hot cooked rice

In 13×9-inch glass baking dish, thoroughly blend onion recipe soup mix, marmalade, orange juice and tarragon; add chicken and turn to coat. Cover and marinate in refrigerator, turning chicken occasionally, at least 4 hours.

Preheat oven to 400°. Bake chicken with marinade, basting and turning chicken occasionally, 1 hour or until done. To serve, arrange chicken over hot rice. If necessary, skim fat from sauce. Serve sauce with chicken. *Makes about 4 servings*

MICROWAVE DIRECTIONS: Marinate chicken as above. Remove chicken from marinade; reserve marinade. In 3-quart casserole, heat chicken, covered, at MEDIUM (50% Full Power) 15 minutes, rearranging chicken once; drain. Add reserved marinade and heat uncovered at HIGH (Full Power) 20 minutes or until chicken is done. Serve as above.

✤ BARBECUED SHRIMP ON A SKEWER

1 envelope Lipton Onion or Onion-Mushroom Recipe Soup Mix
1 can (14½ ounces) whole peeled tomatoes, undrained and chopped
½ cup vegetable or olive oil
¼ cup dry white wine or vermouth
¼ cup chopped fresh basil leaves*
1 tablespoon lemon juice
1 teaspoon cracked peppercorns
2 pounds uncooked large shrimp, cleaned
4 thin slices cooked ham, cut into strips
1 tablespoon finely chopped parsley

In large bowl, combine onion recipe soup mix, tomatoes, oil, wine, basil, lemon juice and peppercorns. Add shrimp. Cover and marinate in refrigerator, stirring occasionally, at least 2 hours. Remove shrimp, reserving marinade.

On skewers, alternately thread shrimp with ham strips, weaving ham around shrimp. Grill or broil, turning and basting frequently with reserved marinade, until shrimp are done. Bring remaining marinade to a boil, then simmer 2 minutes; stir in parsley. Serve as a dipping sauce or, if desired, arrange skewers over hot cooked rice and top with sauce. *Makes about 6 servings*

*Substitution: Use 1½ teaspoons dried basil leaves.

HOT OFF THE GRILL

● Cleanup is easier if you coat the grill top with vegetable cooking spray before barbecuing.

● If you use a charcoal grill, remember that a fire is ready for cooking when the coals are covered with grey ash—about 20 to 30 minutes after lighting.

● Toss damp hickory chunks, outer onion layers or garlic halves on hot coals for flavorful meats, poultry and fish. Grated orange and lemon peel also add a light touch to fruits and vegetables.

● "Kabob-it" by skewering chunks of fresh melon, pineapple, apples, pears or peaches for a toasted fruit salad. Sprinkle with coconut for grilled "ambrosia."

Savory Onion Cheese Tart

❖ LIPTON ONION BURGERS

1 envelope Lipton Onion, Onion-Mushroom, Beefy
    Onion or Beefy Mushroom Recipe Soup Mix
2 pounds ground beef
1/2 cup water

In large bowl, combine all ingredients; shape into 8
patties. Grill or broil until done. Serve, if desired, on
hamburger rolls.   *Makes 8 servings*

MICROWAVE DIRECTIONS: Prepare patties as above.
In oblong baking dish, arrange 4 patties and heat
uncovered at HIGH (Full Power) 6 minutes, turning
patties once. Repeat with remaining patties. Let stand
covered 5 minutes. Serve as above.

❖ CALICO COLESLAW

1 envelope Lipton Vegetable Recipe Soup Mix
1/2 pint (8 ounces) sour cream
1/4 cup mayonnaise
1 tablespoon apple cider vinegar
2 teaspoons Dijon-style prepared mustard
5 cups shredded green cabbage (about 1/2 medium
    head)
1 small red onion, thinly sliced
1 tablespoon finely chopped parsley
   Pepper to taste

In medium bowl, thoroughly blend vegetable recipe
soup mix, sour cream, mayonnaise, vinegar and
mustard. Toss with remaining ingredients; chill.
        Makes about 4 cups coleslaw

Calico Coleslaw, Lipton Onion Burgers

❖ LIPTON ONION BUTTER

Thoroughly blend 1 envelope Lipton Onion Recipe Soup Mix with 1 container (8 ounces) whipped butter or soft margarine, or ½ pound butter or margarine, softened. Store covered in refrigerator.

Makes about 1¼ cups onion butter

ONION-BUTTERED GRILLED VEGETABLES: Brush Lipton Onion Butter on sliced red onion, eggplant or tomatoes, or corn-on-the-cob, then grill or broil until vegetables are tender.

ONION-BUTTERED BREAD: Spread Lipton Onion Butter between slices of French or Italian bread; wrap in aluminum foil and bake at 375°, 15 to 20 minutes.

ONION-BUTTERED BAKED POTATOES: Top a hot, split baked potato with 1 to 2 tablespoons Lipton Onion Butter.

ONION-BUTTERED WHIPPED POTATOES: Add ¼ cup Lipton Onion Butter and ¼ cup milk to 4 medium cooked potatoes; beat until light and fluffy. **OR,** prepare instant mashed potatoes according to package directions, using twice as much Lipton Onion Butter for butter.

ONION-BUTTERED NOODLES: Toss ½ pound cooked and drained noodles with ¼ cup Lipton Onion Butter.

ONION-BUTTERED SANDWICHES: Use softened Lipton Onion Butter to spread on bread slices when making sandwiches. Especially good with roast beef, cheese, lettuce and tomatoes.

ONION-BUTTERED POPCORN: Toss 2½ quarts popped popcorn with ½ cup melted Lipton Onion Butter.

❖ FRESH FISH IN FOIL

    2 fresh fish fillets (about 1 pound)
    1 can (16 ounces) whole potatoes, drained and cut into halves
 ½ cup sliced carrots
    1 envelope Lipton Golden Onion Recipe Soup Mix
 ½ cup water

For each dinner, place 1 fillet on 1 piece (18 × 18-inch) heavy-duty aluminum foil; top with ½ potatoes and ½ carrots. Blend golden onion recipe soup mix with water, then evenly pour over each dinner. Wrap foil loosely around fillets and vegetables, sealing edges airtight with double fold. Grill or broil, seam side up, over hot coals or high heat, 20 minutes or until fish flakes.

Makes 2 servings

❖ SNAPPY PARTY SNACKS

    6 cups bite-size shredded wheat, rice or corn cereal
 ¾ cup unsalted dry roasted mixed nuts
    1 envelope Lipton Onion Recipe Soup Mix
    6 tablespoons butter or margarine, melted

Preheat oven to 300°.

In large bowl, combine cereal, nuts and onion recipe soup mix. Add butter and toss thoroughly. Turn into shallow baking pan and bake 10 minutes.

Makes 6½ cups snacks

MICROWAVE DIRECTIONS: In large glass bowl, heat butter at HIGH (Full Power) 1 minute; blend in onion recipe soup mix. Stir in remaining ingredients and heat uncovered 2½ minutes; toss thoroughly.

❖ TORTELLINI & VEGETABLE SALAD

    1 pound spinach or egg tortellini
    1 envelope Lipton Vegetable Recipe Soup Mix
 ½ cup mayonnaise
 ¼ cup vegetable or olive oil
    1 tablespoon lemon juice
    2 tablespoons chopped fresh basil leaves*
    1 tablespoon finely chopped parsley
 ¼ teaspoon pepper
 ½ cup sliced green onions
 ½ cup chopped tomato

Cook tortellini according to package directions; drain and rinse with cold water until completely cool.

In medium bowl, blend vegetable recipe soup mix, mayonnaise, oil, lemon juice, basil, parsley and pepper. Toss with tortellini, green onions and tomato; chill.

Makes about 4 cups salad

*Substitution: Use 1 teaspoon dried basil leaves.

❖ COUNTRY-STYLE BAKED BEANS

    1 envelope Lipton Onion, Onion-Mushroom or Beefy Mushroom Recipe Soup Mix
    1 can (24 ounces) pork and beans in tomato sauce
    1 medium apple, chopped
 ¼ cup brown sugar
    1 tablespoon prepared mustard

In large saucepan, combine all ingredients. Cook uncovered over medium heat, stirring occasionally, 20 minutes.

Makes about 6 servings

MICROWAVE DIRECTIONS: In 1½-quart casserole, combine all ingredients. Heat covered at HIGH (Full Power), stirring occasionally, 12 minutes or until bubbling. Let stand covered 5 minutes.

❖ CUCUMBER DILL SALAD

1 envelope Lipton Vegetable Recipe Soup Mix
1/2 pint (8 ounces) sour cream
2 teaspoons red wine vinegar
2 teaspoons Dijon-style or yellow prepared
    mustard
1 teaspoon dill weed
1/8 teaspoon pepper
3 medium cucumbers, peeled and thinly sliced
    (about 5 cups)

In medium bowl, blend all ingredients except
cucumbers. Toss with cucumbers; chill at least 2 hours.
Makes about 4 cups salad

❖ DILLY BEAN SALAD

1 envelope Lipton Onion Recipe Soup Mix
3/4 cup water
1/4 cup red wine vinegar
1/4 cup oil
1/4 cup snipped fresh dill*
1 tablespoon finely chopped parsley
1 small clove garlic, finely chopped
1 pound green beans, cooked**
1 can (16 ounces) chick peas (garbanzos) or red
    kidney beans, rinsed and drained (optional)
2 cups fresh or canned sliced mushrooms

In medium bowl, blend onion recipe soup mix, water
and vinegar. Stir in oil, dill, parsley and garlic. Toss with
remaining ingredients; chill.
Makes about 6 cups salad

*Substitution: Use 1 tablespoon dried dill weed.

**Substitution: Use 2 cans (16 ounces each) cut green
beans, drained.

❖ BARBECUE FRUIT RELISH

1 envelope Lipton Onion or Onion-Mushroom
    Recipe Soup Mix
1 pound peaches or nectarines, cut into 1/2-inch
    pieces
1 cup water
1/2 cup raisins
1/2 cup light brown sugar
2 tablespoons apple cider vinegar
2 tablespoons lemon juice
1/2 teaspoon dry mustard
1/4 teaspoon ground allspice
1/4 teaspoon ground ginger

In large saucepan, combine all ingredients. Bring to a
boil, then simmer, stirring occasionally, 40 minutes or
until slightly thickened. Serve warm or cold with grilled
or broiled foods.   *Makes about 2 1/2 cups relish*

❖ MARINATED FLANK STEAK

1 envelope Lipton Onion or Onion-Mushroom
    Recipe Soup Mix
1/2 cup water
1/2 cup dry red wine
1/4 cup olive or vegetable oil
1 tablespoon finely chopped parsley
1 teaspoon oregano
1/8 teaspoon pepper
2-pound beef flank steak

In large shallow baking dish, thoroughly blend all
ingredients except steak; add steak and turn to coat.
Cover and marinate in refrigerator, turning steak and
piercing with fork occasionally, at least 4 hours.
Remove steak, reserving marinade.

Grill or broil steak, turning once, until done. Meanwhile,
in small saucepan, bring remaining marinade to a boil,
then simmer 5 minutes. If necessary, skim fat from
marinade. Serve hot marinade with steak.
Makes about 8 servings

❖ SWEET 'N SPICY ONION TOPPING

1/2 cup butter or margarine
6 medium onions, thinly sliced (about 6 cups)
2/3 cup water
1/2 cup ketchup
1/2 cup sweet pickle relish
1 envelope Lipton Onion, Onion-Mushroom, Beefy
    Mushroom or Beefy Onion Recipe Soup Mix

In large skillet, melt butter and cook onions over
medium heat, stirring occasionally, 35 minutes or until
tender and translucent. Stir in remaining ingredients
and simmer until heated through. Serve with
hamburgers, hot dogs and assorted grilled foods.
Makes about 2 1/2 cups topping

MICROWAVE DIRECTIONS: In 3-quart casserole,
heat butter at HIGH (Full Power) 2 minutes. Add onions
and heat covered, stirring occasionally, 12 minutes or
until tender and translucent. Stir in remaining
ingredients and heat uncovered 10 minutes, stirring
once. Serve as above.

Dilly Bean Salad
Cucumber Dill Salad

✤ BASIL & VEGETABLE CHEESE SPREAD

2 packages (8 ounces each) cream cheese, softened
1/2 cup butter or margarine, softened
1 envelope Lipton Vegetable Recipe Soup Mix
1/4 cup chopped fresh basil leaves*
2 tablespoons grated Parmesan cheese
1/3 cup chopped almonds

Line 7 1/2 × 3 3/4 × 2 1/4-inch loaf pan or small bowl with wax paper or dampened cheesecloth; set aside.

With food processor or electric mixer, combine cream cheese with butter until smooth. Add remaining ingredients; combine until well blended. Pack into prepared pan; cover and chill 2 hours or until firm. To serve, unmold onto serving platter, then remove wax paper. Serve with bagel chips, black bread, cucumber slices or assorted crackers, and fresh fruit.

Makes about 2 3/4 cups spread

*Substitution: Use 2 tablespoons dried basil leaves.

✤ SHISH KABOBS

1 envelope Lipton Golden Onion or Onion Recipe Soup Mix
1/2 pint (8 ounces) plain yogurt
1/4 cup oil
1 teaspoon chili powder
1 teaspoon ground cumin
1/2 teaspoon ground ginger
1 pound boneless lamb or chicken breasts, cut into 1-inch cubes
1 medium green pepper, cut into 1-inch pieces
4 large mushrooms, quartered
1 1/2 cups cubed eggplant (about 1/4 medium)

In large bowl, blend golden onion recipe soup mix, yogurt, oil, chili powder, cumin and ginger. Stir in lamb. Cover and marinate in refrigerator, stirring occasionally, at least 2 hours. Remove lamb, reserving marinade.

On skewers, alternately thread lamb with vegetables. Grill or broil, turning and basting frequently with reserved marinade, until done.

Makes about 4 servings

✤ COUNTRY-STYLE CHICKEN LIVER PÂTÉ

1/4 cup butter or margarine
1 pound chicken livers, rinsed and drained
2 tablespoons Cognac or brandy
1 envelope Lipton Onion or Onion-Mushroom Recipe Soup Mix
1 cup (1/2 pint) whipping or heavy cream
1/2 teaspoon ground allspice (optional)
1/8 teaspoon pepper

In large skillet, melt butter and cook livers over medium heat, stirring frequently, 5 minutes or until done. Stir in Cognac and simmer 2 minutes.

In food processor or blender, process liver mixture with remaining ingredients until smooth. Pack into small bowl; cover and chill at least 2 hours. Serve with assorted crackers or sliced breads.

Makes about 2 cups pâté

✤ 6-FOOT SOUPER SANDWICH

1 envelope Lipton Golden Onion Recipe Soup Mix
1 pint (16 ounces) sour cream
1/4 cup prepared mustard
1 loaf French or Italian bread (about 6 feet long), cut in half lengthwise*
2 pounds sliced cooked turkey
2 pounds sliced cooked roast beef
1 1/2 pounds sliced Swiss or American cheese
2 medium tomatoes, sliced
2 medium avocados, sliced
Lettuce leaves

In medium bowl, blend golden onion recipe soup mix, sour cream and mustard; chill.

Spread mixture evenly on each bread half. On bottom bread half, layer turkey, roast beef and cheese. Top 1/2 of sandwich with tomatoes and the other 1/2 with avocados; top with lettuce, then remaining bread half.

Makes about 20 servings

*Substitution: Use 6 loaves French or Italian bread (about 16 inches long), cut in half lengthwise. Cut rounded ends as needed and place loaves end to end.

Basil & Vegetable Cheese Spread

IMPROMPTU GET-TOGETHERS

❖ BAGELS 'N CREAM CHEESE SPREADS

1/2 pint (8 ounces) sour cream
1 package (8 ounces) cream cheese, softened
   Flavor Choices* (choose one)
   Assorted bagels, halved

In medium bowl, blend sour cream with cream cheese. Stir in 1 Flavor Choice; cover and chill at least 2 hours. Top bagel halves with spread.

Makes about 2 cups spread

*Flavor Choices—
● **ONION-CARAWAY SPREAD:** Blend in 1 envelope Lipton Onion Recipe Soup Mix, 2 tablespoons milk, 1 tablespoon prepared mustard and 1 teaspoon caraway seeds.

● **RAISIN-WALNUT SPREAD:** Blend in 1 envelope Lipton Vegetable Recipe Soup Mix, 1/2 cup chopped walnuts and 1/2 cup raisins.

● **SMOKED SALMON 'N DILL SPREAD:** Blend in 1 envelope Lipton Golden Onion Recipe Soup Mix, 4 ounces smoked salmon, chopped, and 1 teaspoon dill weed.

❖ PACK A POCKET SANDWICH

1 envelope Lipton Golden Onion Recipe Soup Mix
1/2 pint (8 ounces) plain yogurt
1/4 teaspoon ground ginger
2 cups cut-up cooked chicken
1/2 cup chopped water chestnuts*
4 large pita breads, halved
4 ounces snow peas
3 cups fresh or canned bean sprouts

In medium bowl, blend golden onion recipe soup mix, yogurt and ginger. Stir in chicken and water chestnuts; chill. To serve, line pita breads with snow peas, then fill with chicken mixture and top with bean sprouts.

Makes about 4 servings

*Substitution: Use 1/2 cup chopped unsalted cashews.

❖ DELUXE NACHO POTATO SKINS

1 pound ground beef
1 envelope Lipton Onion or Onion-Mushroom
   Recipe Soup Mix
1/2 cup water
1 can (4 ounces) chopped green chilies, undrained
1 teaspoon chili powder
1/2 teaspoon ground cumin (optional)
1 medium tomato, chopped
2 packages (10 to 12 ounces each) frozen potato
   skins
1 cup shredded Cheddar cheese (about 4 ounces)

Preheat oven to 425°.

In medium skillet, brown ground beef over medium-high heat; drain. Stir in onion recipe soup mix, water, chilies, chili powder, cumin and tomato. Simmer uncovered, stirring occasionally, 10 minutes.

In shallow baking pan, arrange potato skins; evenly top with ground beef mixture, then cheese. Bake 10 minutes or until potato skins are done and cheese is melted. Serve, if desired, with sour cream and guacamole. *Makes about 30 potato skins*

MICROWAVE DIRECTIONS: In 2-quart casserole, heat ground beef, uncovered, at HIGH (Full Power) 4 minutes, stirring once; drain. Stir in onion recipe soup mix, water, chilies, chili powder, cumin and tomato. Heat uncovered 4 minutes, stirring once. In 2-quart oblong baking dish, arrange 1/2 potato skins; evenly top with 1/2 ground beef mixture. Heat uncovered 5 minutes, rearranging potatoes once. Top with 1/2 cheese, then heat 1 minute or until cheese is melted. Repeat with remaining potato skins. Serve warm and, if desired, as above.

Bagels 'n Cream Cheese Spreads
Clockwise from top right:
Raisin-Walnut Spread
Smoked Salmon 'n Dill Spread
Onion-Caraway Spread

❖ SEAFOOD SALAD SANDWICHES

1 envelope Lipton Vegetable Recipe Soup Mix
3/4 cup sour cream
1/4 cup mayonnaise
1 teaspoon lemon juice
1/2 cup chopped celery
1 tablespoon fresh or frozen chopped chives (optional)
Hot pepper sauce to taste
1/8 teaspoon pepper
2 packages (6 ounces each) frozen crabmeat, thawed and well drained*
4 hard rolls, halved
Lettuce leaves

In large bowl, blend vegetable recipe soup mix, sour cream, mayonnaise, lemon juice, celery, chives, hot pepper sauce and pepper. Stir in crabmeat; chill. To serve, line rolls with lettuce, then fill with crab mixture.

Makes 4 hearty sandwiches

*Variations: Use 1 package (12 ounces) frozen cleaned shrimp, cooked and coarsely chopped; **OR** 2 packages (8 ounces each) sea legs, thawed, drained and chopped; **OR** 1 can (13 ounces) tuna, drained and flaked; **OR** 2 cans (4 1/2 ounces each) medium or large shrimp, drained and chopped; **OR** 2 cans (6 1/2 ounces each) crabmeat, drained and flaked.

❖ GOLDEN BREADED TURKEY CUTLETS

1 envelope Lipton Onion or Golden Onion Recipe Soup Mix
3/4 cup plain dry bread crumbs
1/4 cup grated Parmesan cheese
1 teaspoon dry mustard
1 1/2 pounds boneless turkey or chicken breasts, pounded 1/4 inch thick
1/4 cup all-purpose flour
2 eggs, slightly beaten
1/4 cup butter or margarine, melted

Preheat oven to 350°.

In medium bowl, thoroughly combine onion recipe soup mix, bread crumbs, cheese and mustard. Dip turkey in flour, then eggs, then bread crumb mixture, coating well. In lightly greased large shallow baking pan, arrange turkey, then drizzle with butter. Bake, turning once, 20 minutes or until done.

Makes about 4 servings

❖ SIMPLY DELICIOUS PRIMAVERA

1 envelope Lipton Vegetable Recipe Soup Mix
1 1/2 teaspoons all-purpose flour
1 1/2 cups milk
1/4 cup butter or margarine
2 tablespoons grated Parmesan cheese
8 ounces linguine or spaghetti, cooked and drained

Blend vegetable recipe soup mix, flour and milk. In medium saucepan, melt butter and stir in milk mixture. Bring just to the boiling point, then simmer, stirring occasionally, until sauce is thickened and vegetables are tender, about 10 minutes. Stir in cheese. Toss sauce with hot linguine and sprinkle, if desired, with additional Parmesan cheese.

Makes about 4 servings

MICROWAVE DIRECTIONS: In 1-quart casserole, heat butter at HIGH (Full Power) 2 minutes. Stir in vegetable recipe soup mix and flour blended with milk. Heat uncovered, stirring occasionally, 7 minutes or until sauce is thickened and vegetables are tender. Stir in cheese. Toss as above.

❖ ZUCCHINI FRITTATA SANDWICHES

1 envelope Lipton Golden Onion Recipe Soup Mix
6 eggs
1/2 cup milk
1/2 teaspoon oregano
1/8 teaspoon pepper
1/2 cup shredded mozzarella cheese (about 1 1/2 ounces)
2 tablespoons butter or margarine
2 cups thinly sliced zucchini (about 1 large)
6 hard rolls or croissants*

In medium bowl, beat golden onion recipe soup mix, eggs, milk, oregano and pepper. Stir in cheese; set aside.

In medium skillet, melt butter and cook zucchini over medium heat, stirring frequently, 3 minutes or until almost tender. Add egg mixture and cook covered over low heat 20 minutes or until set. Cut into 6 wedges and serve in rolls.

Makes 6 servings

*Substitution: Use 12 thick slices Italian or French bread.

MICROWAVE DIRECTIONS: Prepare egg mixture as above. In 2-quart casserole, heat butter with zucchini, uncovered, at HIGH (Full Power) 4 minutes. Add egg mixture and heat covered 3 minutes. With spatula, lift set edges of frittata, tilting casserole to allow uncooked mixture to flow toward edges. Heat covered an additional 3 minutes. Let stand covered 5 minutes. Cut and serve as above.

Seafood Salad Sandwiches

✤ ONION 'N CHEESE SOUFFLÉ

2 tablespoons butter or margarine
2 tablespoons all-purpose flour
1 envelope Lipton Golden Onion Recipe Soup Mix
1¼ cups milk
4 eggs, separated
½ cup shredded Swiss or fontina cheese (about 2 ounces)
1 teaspoon prepared mustard
½ teaspoon caraway seeds
⅛ teaspoon pepper

Preheat oven to 400°.

In large saucepan, melt butter and cook flour over medium heat, stirring constantly, until golden, about 5 minutes. Gradually stir in golden onion recipe soup mix thoroughly blended with milk. Bring just to the boiling point, then simmer, stirring occasionally, 1 minute or until thickened. Remove from heat, then beat in egg yolks, one at a time, beating well after each addition. Stir in cheese, mustard, caraway and pepper.

Beat egg whites until stiff peaks form; gently fold into egg yolk mixture. Turn into well buttered 3- or 4-cup soufflé dish. Bake 25 minutes or until puffed and golden brown. Serve immediately.

Makes about 6 servings

MAKE-AHEAD DIRECTIONS: Soufflé can be partially prepared up to 2 days ahead. Simply prepare as above, but do not beat or add egg whites. Cover and refrigerate base mixture and egg whites separately. To serve, beat egg whites, then continue as above.

✤ FRIED CHICKEN WITH CINNAMON & HONEY DIPPIN' SAUCE

1 package (26 to 32 ounces) frozen fully cooked fried or batter-dipped chicken
1 envelope Lipton Golden Onion Recipe Soup Mix
1¼ cups apple juice
¼ cup honey
½ teaspoon ground cinnamon
½ cup chopped walnuts

Bake chicken according to package directions. Remove to serving platter and keep warm.

Meanwhile, in small saucepan, thoroughly blend golden onion recipe soup mix, apple juice, honey and cinnamon. Bring to a boil, then cook over medium heat, stirring occasionally, 7 minutes or until thickened. Stir in walnuts. Serve as a dipping sauce or pour over chicken.

Makes about 4 servings

NOTE: Cinnamon & Honey Dippin' Sauce is also great with cooked pork, turkey, game, sweet potatoes, acorn squash and carrots.

✤ QUICK 'N EASY TACOS

1 pound ground beef
1 can (14½ ounces) whole peeled tomatoes, undrained and coarsely chopped
1 medium green pepper, finely chopped
1 envelope Lipton Onion, Onion-Mushroom or Beefy Mushroom Recipe Soup Mix
1 tablespoon chili powder
3 drops hot pepper sauce
8 taco shells
Taco Toppings*

In medium skillet, brown ground beef over medium-high heat; drain. Stir in tomatoes, green pepper, onion recipe soup mix, chili powder and hot pepper sauce. Bring to a boil, then simmer 15 minutes or until slightly thickened. Serve in taco shells with assorted Taco Toppings.

Makes about 4 servings

*Taco Toppings: Use shredded Cheddar or Monterey Jack cheese, shredded lettuce, chopped tomatoes, sliced pitted ripe olives, sour cream or taco sauce.

MICROWAVE DIRECTIONS: In 2-quart casserole, heat ground beef with green pepper, uncovered, at HIGH (Full Power) 4 minutes, stirring once; drain. Stir in tomatoes, onion recipe soup mix, chili powder and hot pepper sauce. Heat uncovered, stirring occasionally, 7 minutes or until heated through. Let stand uncovered 5 minutes. Serve as above.

✤ QUICK CORN BREAD WITH CHILIES 'N CHEESE

1 package (12 to 16 ounces) corn bread or corn muffin mix
1 cup shredded Monterey Jack cheese (about 3 ounces)
1 can (4 ounces) chopped green chilies, drained
1 envelope Lipton Vegetable Recipe Soup Mix

Prepare corn bread mix according to package directions; stir in ½ cup cheese, chilies and vegetable recipe soup mix. In lightly greased 8-inch baking pan, bake as directed. While warm, top with remaining cheese; on wire rack, cool completely. To serve, cut into squares.

Makes about 16 squares

*Quick 'n Easy Tacos
Quick Corn Bread with Chilies 'n Cheese*

✤ CHICKEN & BROCCOLI STUFFED POTATOES

    2 tablespoons oil
    1 pound boneless chicken breasts, cut into thin
        strips
    ½ pound broccoli, cut into 1½-inch pieces*
    1 can (8 ounces) water chestnuts, drained and
        sliced
    ½ teaspoon ground ginger
    ¼ teaspoon garlic powder
    1 envelope Lipton Golden Onion Recipe Soup Mix
    1 cup water
    2 tablespoons soy sauce
    6 hot baked large potatoes

In large skillet, heat oil and cook chicken over medium-high heat until almost done. Add broccoli, water chestnuts, ginger and garlic powder. Cook, stirring frequently, 2 minutes. Stir in golden onion recipe soup mix thoroughly blended with water and soy sauce. Bring to a boil, then simmer, stirring occasionally, 5 minutes or until sauce is thickened.

Cut each potato in half lengthwise, almost completely through; mash pulp lightly. Top each potato, if desired, with butter. To serve, evenly spoon chicken mixture into hot potatoes. *Makes 6 servings*

*Substitution: Use 1 package (10 ounces) frozen broccoli spears, thawed and cut into 1½-inch pieces.

✤ ORIENTAL PEPPER STEAK

    2 tablespoons oil
    1 pound boneless chuck or round steak, cut into
        thin strips
    1 envelope Lipton Onion, Onion-Mushroom, Beefy
        Onion or Beefy Mushroom Recipe Soup Mix
    2 cups water
    1 medium green pepper, cut into thin strips
    2 teaspoons soy sauce
    ½ teaspoon ground ginger
    1 medium clove garlic, finely chopped
    1 medium tomato, cut into wedges
    1 tablespoon cornstarch
      Hot cooked rice

In large skillet, heat oil and brown beef over medium-high heat; drain. Stir in onion recipe soup mix blended with 1½ cups water. Bring to a boil, then simmer covered 20 minutes. Stir in green pepper, soy sauce, ginger and garlic. Simmer covered 15 minutes or until beef is tender. Stir in tomato, then cornstarch blended with remaining water. Bring to a boil, then simmer, stirring constantly, until sauce is thickened, about 5 minutes. To serve, arrange beef mixture over hot rice.
Makes about 4 servings

✤ POLYNESIAN CHICKEN WITH RICE

    2 tablespoons oil
    1 pound boneless chicken breasts, cut into thin
        strips
    1 can (8 ounces) pineapple chunks in natural juice,
        undrained
    1 medium green pepper, cut into thin strips
    1 envelope Lipton Golden Onion Recipe Soup Mix
    ¾ cup water
    2 teaspoons soy sauce
    ¼ teaspoon ground ginger
    ½ cup unsalted cashews (optional)
      Hot cooked rice

In large skillet, heat oil and brown chicken over medium-high heat. Stir in pineapple and green pepper, then golden onion recipe soup mix thoroughly blended with water, soy sauce and ginger. Bring to a boil, then simmer uncovered, stirring occasionally, 10 minutes or until chicken is done. Stir in cashews. To serve, arrange chicken mixture over hot rice and top, if desired, with flaked coconut. *Makes about 4 servings*

MICROWAVE DIRECTIONS: Omit oil and decrease ginger to a generous dash. In 2-quart casserole, heat chicken, uncovered, at HIGH (Full Power) 3 minutes, stirring once. Remove chicken and drain. Add pineapple and green pepper, then golden onion recipe soup mix thoroughly blended with water, soy sauce and ginger. Heat covered, stirring occasionally, 6 minutes or until sauce is thickened. Return chicken to casserole and heat 1 minute or until chicken is done. Let stand covered 5 minutes. Stir in cashews. Serve as above.

✤ TEMPTING TACO BURGERS

    1 envelope Lipton Onion-Mushroom, Onion, Beefy
        Onion or Beefy Mushroom Recipe Soup Mix
    1 pound ground beef
    ½ cup chopped tomato
    ¼ cup finely chopped green pepper
    1 teaspoon chili powder
    ¼ cup water

In large bowl, combine all ingredients; shape into 4 patties. Grill or broil until done. Serve, if desired, on hamburger rolls and top with shredded lettuce and Cheddar cheese. *Makes about 4 servings*

MICROWAVE DIRECTIONS: Prepare patties as above. In oblong baking dish, arrange patties and heat uncovered at HIGH (Full Power) 10 minutes, turning patties once. Let stand covered 5 minutes. Serve as above.

Chicken & Broccoli Stuffed Potatoes

FORMAL AFFAIRS

❖ VEAL SCALLOPINI WITH BRANDY CREAM SAUCE

1 pound veal scallopini, pounded 1/4 inch thick
   (about 4 cutlets)
1/4 cup all-purpose flour
3 tablespoons butter or margarine
1 medium apple, thinly sliced
1 envelope Lipton Golden Onion Recipe Soup Mix
1 1/2 cups water
2 tablespoons brandy
1/2 cup light cream or half and half
1 tablespoon light brown sugar

Lightly coat veal with flour.

In large skillet, melt butter and cook veal over medium heat until tender. Remove veal to serving platter and keep warm. Reserve 1 tablespoon drippings. Add apple, then golden onion recipe soup mix thoroughly blended with water and brandy to reserved drippings. Bring to a boil, then simmer, stirring occasionally, 10 minutes. Stir in cream and sugar and heat through. Serve sauce over veal.
Makes about 4 servings

❖ CHICKEN CORDON BLEU WITH GOLDEN CREAM SAUCE

3 whole boneless chicken breasts (about 2 1/2
   pounds), halved and lightly pounded
6 slices Swiss cheese
6 slices cooked ham
2 tablespoons butter or margarine
1/4 teaspoon ground nutmeg
1/8 teaspoon pepper
1 envelope Lipton Golden Onion Recipe Soup Mix
2 cups (1 pint) light cream or half and half
1/4 cup water
   Hot cooked noodles

Top each chicken breast half with slice of cheese and ham; roll up and secure with wooden toothpicks.

In large skillet, melt butter and brown chicken over medium heat; drain. Add nutmeg and pepper, then golden onion recipe soup mix blended with cream and water. Bring just to the boiling point, then simmer covered, basting occasionally, 20 minutes or until chicken is done. To serve, arrange chicken and sauce over hot noodles.
Makes about 6 servings

❖ CROWN ROAST OF PORK WITH COGNAC GLAZE

1 cup orange juice
1 jar (12 ounces) red currant or grape jelly
1 envelope Lipton Onion or Onion-Mushroom
   Recipe Soup Mix
1/2 cup Cognac or brandy
1/2 teaspoon ground ginger
8- to 9-pound crown roast of pork (about 22 ribs)
   Warm Dried Fruit Compote (recipe follows)

Preheat oven to 200°.

In medium saucepan, heat orange juice, jelly, onion recipe soup mix, Cognac and ginger over low heat, stirring occasionally, 5 minutes or until jelly is melted.

In roasting pan, place crown roast; brush with jelly glaze, then pour remaining glaze over roast. Loosely cover with heavy-duty aluminum foil; roast 2 hours. Increase heat to 350° and continue roasting, basting occasionally, an additional 1 1/2 hours or until meat thermometer reaches 175°. Remove foil and continue roasting, basting occasionally and adding water if needed, 20 minutes or until thermometer reaches 180°.

Remove roast to serving platter and keep warm. Skim fat from pan drippings and serve pan juices with roast. Spoon Warm Dried Fruit Compote into center cavity and around roast.
Makes about 12 servings

WARM DRIED FRUIT COMPOTE

In large saucepan, combine 2 cups dried apricots, 2 cups pitted dried prunes, 12 dried figs, halved,* 2 cups orange juice, 2 tablespoons fresh squeezed lemon juice, 3 cinnamon sticks and 1 teaspoon whole cloves. Bring to a boil, then simmer 5 minutes. Stir in 1 cup green or red seedless grapes and simmer 2 minutes or until heated through. Remove cinnamon.
Makes about 8 cups

*Substitution: Use 2 packages (11 ounces each) pitted mixed dried fruit instead of apricots, prunes and figs.

MAKE-AHEAD DIRECTIONS FOR COMPOTE:
Compote can be prepared up to 2 days ahead. Simply combine as above; bring to a boil, then simmer 5 minutes. Cover and refrigerate. Just before serving, heat through; stir in grapes, then continue as above.

Crown Roast of Pork with Cognac Glaze

❖ ROASTED CHICKEN WITH BROCCOLI & CAULIFLOWER

1 envelope Lipton Golden Onion or Onion Recipe Soup Mix
1/2 cup butter or margarine, melted
1/2 teaspoon tarragon leaves
4- to 5-pound roasting chicken, stuffed*
1 medium bunch broccoli, separated into large florets
1 medium head cauliflower, separated into large florets
1/4 cup sliced almonds
1 cup cherry tomatoes

Preheat oven to 350°. Blend golden onion recipe soup mix, butter and tarragon; set aside.

In large roasting pan, place chicken; brush with 1/4 butter mixture. Roast uncovered 1 1/2 hours, basting once. Arrange broccoli and cauliflower around chicken, then top with almonds; brush with remaining butter mixture. Loosely cover with heavy-duty aluminum foil; roast 30 minutes. Add tomatoes, then baste. Roast uncovered, basting occasionally, an additional 10 minutes or until meat thermometer reaches 185°. If necessary, continue roasting vegetables, covered, until tender. To serve, on large serving platter, arrange chicken and vegetables.   *Makes about 6 servings*

*Use 2 cups of your favorite stuffing.

❖ ROASTED LEG OF LAMB WITH LEMON-ROSEMARY GLAZE

5- to 6-pound leg of lamb
6 large cloves garlic, halved
4 large sprigs fresh rosemary, torn into pieces*
1/2 teaspoon pepper
1/4 cup butter or margarine, melted
1 can (6 ounces) frozen lemonade concentrate, partially thawed and undiluted
1 envelope Lipton Onion or Onion-Mushroom Recipe Soup Mix

Preheat oven to 325°.

In roasting pan, place lamb fat side up. With knife, make several 1-inch-deep cuts in lamb; stuff cuts with garlic and 1/2 of the rosemary. Sprinkle with pepper, then drizzle with butter. Roast 1 hour or until meat thermometer reaches 140°.

Meanwhile, in small bowl, blend lemonade concentrate, onion recipe soup mix and remaining rosemary. Pour over lamb, then continue roasting, basting occasionally, 30 minutes or until thermometer reaches 145°.

Remove lamb to serving platter and keep warm. Skim fat from pan drippings and serve pan juices with lamb. Garnish, if desired, with additional rosemary and lemon slices.   *Makes about 10 servings*

*Substitution: Use 1 tablespoon dried rosemary leaves.

Roasted Chicken with Broccoli & Cauliflower

❖ STANDING RIB ROAST WITH MADEIRA SAUCE

2 large cloves garlic, finely chopped
1 teaspoon marjoram leaves (optional)
1 teaspoon thyme leaves
1 teaspoon salt
1/4 teaspoon pepper
5-pound standing rib roast (about 3 ribs)
1/4 cup butter or margarine
2 cups thinly sliced mushrooms
1/4 cup Madeira or dry red wine
1 tablespoon tomato paste
1 envelope Lipton Onion, Onion-Mushroom or
   Beefy Mushroom Recipe Soup Mix
1 tablespoon all-purpose flour
1 1/2 cups water
1 tablespoon finely chopped parsley
   Pepper to taste

Preheat oven to 500°. In small bowl, combine garlic, marjoram, thyme, salt and pepper; set aside.

Trim fat from roast. In roasting pan, on rack, place roast; rub with garlic mixture. Roast 10 minutes, then decrease heat to 350° and continue roasting 1 1/2 hours or until meat thermometer reaches 130° (rare) or 150° (medium).

Remove roast to serving platter and keep warm. Skim fat from pan drippings. In medium saucepan, combine pan juices with butter; stir in mushrooms. Cook 5 minutes or until mushrooms are tender. Stir in wine and tomato paste, then onion recipe soup mix and flour blended with water. Bring to a boil, then simmer, stirring frequently, 5 minutes or until sauce is thickened. Stir in parsley and pepper. Serve sauce with roast. *Makes about 6 servings*

❖ CREAMY CHICKEN TARRAGON

2 tablespoons oil
2 1/2- to 3-pound chicken, cut into serving pieces
1 envelope Lipton Onion, Onion-Mushroom or
   Golden Onion Recipe Soup Mix
1/2 teaspoon tarragon leaves
1 cup water
1/2 cup dry white wine
2 tablespoons all-purpose flour
1/2 cup whipping or heavy cream

In large skillet, heat oil and brown chicken over medium-high heat; drain. Add onion recipe soup mix and tarragon blended with water and wine. Simmer covered 45 minutes or until chicken is done. Remove chicken to serving platter and keep warm. Into skillet, stir in flour blended with cream. Bring just to the boiling point, then simmer, stirring constantly, until sauce is thickened, about 5 minutes. Serve sauce over chicken. *Makes about 4 servings*

MICROWAVE DIRECTIONS: Omit oil. In 3-quart casserole, heat chicken, uncovered, at HIGH (Full Power) 12 minutes, rearranging chicken once; drain. Add onion recipe soup mix and tarragon blended with water and wine. Heat covered 14 minutes or until chicken is done, rearranging chicken once. Remove chicken to serving platter and keep warm. Into casserole, stir flour blended with cream and heat uncovered 4 minutes or until sauce is thickened, stirring once. Serve as above.

THE GOURMET TOUCH

Even the busiest cook can take time to create these special touches.

SPECIAL LEMON WEDGES: Dip lemon wedges into finely chopped fresh green herbs to create a colorful garnish.

THE PROFESSIONAL TOUCH: Use a pastry bag to pipe out creamy spreads or dips, whipped butter or cream, etc. A 12-inch bag with a number 8 star tip is the most versatile.

CHOCOLATE-DIPPED STRAWBERRIES: Wash and thoroughly dry 1 pint strawberries, leaving stems intact. In double boiler or heavy-duty saucepan, over low heat melt 3 ounces semi-sweet chocolate with 1 tablespoon solid shortening. Dip fruit halfway into chocolate. Place on wax paper and refrigerate to harden. Place in candy cups. Best if served within 12 hours.

CHOCOLATE LEAVES: Brush undersides of mint or rose leaves with melted chocolate; refrigerate. When the chocolate is firm, carefully pull the leaf away and use the chocolate "leaf" to decorate cakes or desserts.

HOMEMADE CORDIALS: In 3-quart glass jar with a lid, combine 1 quart vodka, 2 pints fresh cherries, raspberries or strawberries, and 2 cups sugar; cover. Store in a cool, dark place for at least 2 months, stirring once each week. To serve, strain liquid through a fine sieve. Store covered. Use fruit as a dessert topping.

FRESH HERB VINEGAR: In 1-quart glass bottle or jar, combine 2 cups vinegar (white, white wine or cider) and 1 cup loosely packed fresh herbs such as basil, tarragon, chives or dill, thoroughly washed. If desired, add lemon peel or a garlic clove. Cover and let stand a few days, then strain into a clean bottle or jar. Store covered.

STOP 'N GO FOODS

APPETIZERS = ENTRÉES

❖ GOLDEN CHICKEN NUGGETS

1 envelope Lipton Golden Onion Recipe Soup Mix
3/4 cup plain dry bread crumbs
1 1/2 pounds boneless chicken breasts, cut into 1-inch pieces
1/4 cup butter or margarine, melted

Preheat oven to 400°. Combine golden onion recipe soup mix with bread crumbs. Dip chicken in bread crumbs mixture, coating well. In lightly greased large shallow baking pan, arrange chicken, then drizzle with butter. Bake, turning once, 10 minutes or until chicken is done. *Makes about 2 dozen nuggets*

❖ SHRIMP 'N POTATO BITES

1 envelope Lipton Onion or Golden Onion Recipe Soup Mix
2 cups mashed potatoes, chilled
2 cups coarsely chopped cooked or canned shrimp
1 cup shredded Muenster or mozzarella cheese (about 3 ounces)
1 cup plain dry bread crumbs
1 egg, slightly beaten
1/8 teaspoon pepper
Oil

In large bowl, thoroughly combine onion recipe soup mix, potatoes, shrimp, cheese, 1/2 cup bread crumbs, egg and pepper. Shape into 1 1/2-inch balls, then roll in remaining bread crumbs. Chill at least 2 hours.

In deep-fat fryer, heat oil to 375°. Carefully drop shrimp balls into hot oil and fry until golden brown; drain on paper towels. Serve warm.
Makes about 3 dozen shrimp bites

❖ CHICKEN WINGS WITH HONEY & ORANGE SAUCE

12 chicken wings (about 2 pounds)
1 envelope Lipton Golden Onion Recipe Soup Mix
1/3 cup honey
1/4 cup water
1/4 cup frozen concentrated orange juice, partially thawed and undiluted
1/4 cup sherry
1 tablespoon prepared mustard
2 teaspoons soy sauce
1/4 teaspoon ground ginger
3 dashes hot pepper sauce

Preheat oven to 350°.

Cut tips off chicken wings (save tips for soup). Halve remaining chicken wings at joint.

In 13 × 9-inch baking dish, blend remaining ingredients; add chicken and turn to coat. Bake uncovered, basting occasionally, 40 minutes or until chicken is done and sauce is thickened. *Makes 24 appetizers*

MICROWAVE DIRECTIONS: In 13 × 9-inch baking dish, prepare chicken wings and sauce as above. Heat uncovered at HIGH (Full Power), basting and rearranging chicken occasionally, 20 minutes or until chicken is done and sauce is thickened. Let stand uncovered 5 minutes.

Chicken Wings with Honey & Orange Sauce

❖ HOT SEAFOOD DIP-IN

    1 envelope Lipton Vegetable Recipe Soup Mix
    1 cup olive or vegetable oil
    2 tablespoons lemon juice
    1 tablespoon prepared mustard
    1 egg
    1 large clove garlic, chopped
 1/8 teaspoon pepper
    Suggested Seafood Dippers*

In food processor or blender, combine vegetable recipe soup mix, 1/4 cup oil, lemon juice, mustard, egg, garlic and pepper. While processing, through feed cap, add remaining oil in a thin steady stream; process until mixture is thickened. Serve immediately or cover and chill. To serve, arrange Suggested Seafood Dippers around dip.   *Makes about 1 1/2 cups dip*

*Suggested Seafood Dippers: Use hot cooked shrimp, scallops, crab or lobster. Also great with hot cooked broccoli florets, cauliflowerets, carrots and new potatoes.

❖ THICK 'N CHEESY VEGETABLE PIZZA

    2 loaves (1 pound each) frozen bread dough, thawed
    1 envelope Lipton Vegetable Recipe Soup Mix
 1/4 cup olive or vegetable oil
    2 tablespoons chopped fresh basil leaves*
    1 large clove garlic, finely chopped
 1/4 teaspoon pepper
    2 cups shredded mozzarella cheese (about 6 ounces)
    1 cup fresh or canned sliced mushrooms
    1 medium tomato, coarsely chopped

Preheat oven to 425°.

Into lightly oiled 12-inch pizza pan, press dough to form crust; set aside.

In small bowl, blend vegetable recipe soup mix, oil, basil, garlic and pepper; spread evenly on dough. Top with remaining ingredients. Bake 20 minutes or until cheese is melted and crust is golden brown. To serve, cut into wedges.   *Makes about 6 servings*

*Substitution: Use 2 teaspoons dried basil leaves.

Thick 'n Cheesy Vegetable Pizza

❖ SWEET 'N SOUR MEATBALLS

    1 envelope Lipton Beefy Onion Recipe Soup Mix
1½ pounds ground beef
    ½ cup fresh bread crumbs
    1 egg
    2 tablespoons brown sugar
1½ tablespoons cornstarch
    1 can (20 ounces) pineapple chunks in natural
         juice, drained (reserve juice)
    ¼ cup vinegar
    ¼ cup water
    2 green peppers, cut into chunks

In large bowl, combine beefy onion recipe soup mix, ground beef, bread crumbs and egg; shape into 1-inch meatballs.

In large skillet, cook meatballs over medium heat. Remove meatballs to serving dish and keep warm. Into skillet, add sugar and cornstarch blended with reserved juice, vinegar and water. Stir in pineapple and green peppers. Bring to a boil, then simmer, stirring constantly, until sauce is thickened, about 5 minutes. Serve sauce over meatballs.

Makes about 5 dozen meatballs

MICROWAVE DIRECTIONS: Prepare and shape meatballs as above. In 3-quart casserole, blend sugar, cornstarch, reserved juice, vinegar and water; add green peppers. Heat covered at HIGH (Full Power) 8 minutes or until sauce is thickened, stirring once. Stir in meatballs and pineapple. Heat covered, stirring occasionally, 8 minutes or until meatballs are done. Let stand covered 5 minutes.

❖ MEXICALI NACHO PLATTER

    1 envelope Lipton Nacho Cheese Recipe Soup Mix
1¼ cups milk
    1 pound boneless chicken breasts, cooked and cut
         into thin strips
    Corn tortilla or nacho chips
    Assorted Nacho Toppings*

In 2-quart saucepan, with wire whip or fork, thoroughly blend nacho cheese recipe soup mix with milk. Bring just to the boiling point, stirring frequently, then reduce heat and simmer covered, stirring occasionally, 5 minutes. Stir in chicken and heat through. To serve, arrange chips on large serving platter. Top with ½ nacho sauce and Assorted Nacho Toppings, then add remaining sauce and toppings.

Makes about 4 main-dish servings

*Assorted Nacho Toppings: Use any combination of the following—sliced pitted ripe olives; chopped green onions, tomatoes, green chilies and avocado; and crumbled cooked bacon.

❖ VEGETABLE 'N PORK FILLED WONTONS

    1 envelope Lipton Vegetable Recipe Soup Mix
    ½ pound ground pork or beef
    1 cup fresh or canned bean sprouts
    3 ounces spinach leaves, chopped (about 2 cups)*
    1 tablespoon sherry
    ½ teaspoon ground ginger
    1 package (16 ounces) refrigerated wonton
         wrappers (about 50 wrappers)
    Oil

In medium bowl, thoroughly combine vegetable recipe soup mix, ground pork, bean sprouts, spinach, sherry and ginger. Place 1 teaspoon pork mixture on center of each wrapper; gather edges of wrapper around filling and press firmly at top to seal.

In deep-fat fryer, heat oil to 375°. Carefully drop wontons in hot oil and fry until golden brown; drain on paper towels. Serve warm and, if desired, with assorted mustards or duck sauce.   *Makes about 50 wontons*

*Substitution: Use 1 package (10 ounces) frozen chopped spinach, cooked and squeezed dry.

FREEZING DIRECTIONS: Wontons can be frozen up to 1 month. Simply prepare as above, but do not fry. Arrange on cookie sheet and freeze uncovered 1 hour, then wrap in heavy-duty aluminum foil; freeze. To serve, partially thaw, then fry as above.

❖ GOLDEN MINI QUICHES

    1 envelope Lipton Golden Onion Recipe Soup Mix
1½ cups light cream or half and half
    3 eggs, beaten
    Pastry for double-crust pie*
    1 cup shredded Swiss cheese (about 4 ounces)

Preheat oven to 400°.

In medium bowl, thoroughly blend golden onion recipe soup mix, cream and eggs; set aside.

On lightly floured board, roll pastry ⅛ inch thick; cut into 36 (2½-inch) circles. Press into 7½ × 9¾-inch muffin pans. Evenly fill prepared pans with cheese, then egg mixture. Bake 25 minutes or until knife inserted in center comes out clean and pastry is golden. Serve warm.   *Makes 3 dozen mini quiches*

*Variation: For one 9-inch quiche, bake one 9-inch unbaked pastry shell at 375°, 10 minutes. Fill pastry shell with cheese, then egg mixture. Bake 40 minutes or until quiche tests done and pastry is golden. *Makes about 8 servings.*

FREEZING/REHEATING DIRECTIONS: Mini quiches can be baked, then frozen. Simply wrap in heavy-duty aluminum foil; freeze. To reheat, unwrap and bake at 350°, 15 minutes or until heated through. **OR,** place 12 quiches on plate and microwave at HIGH (Full Power) 4 minutes or until heated through, turning plate once.

SOUP AND...

QUICK-TO-FIX MEAL

Lipton Hearty Noodle Soup Mix
with Vegetables in Real Chicken Broth

Chunky Chicken Salad
with Almonds & Grapes*

Whole Grain Bread

Fruit Sorbet with Mint

Cranberry Juice Cocktail with Lime

ON-THE-GO SOUP 'N SANDWICH SUPPER

Lipton Hearty Beefy Noodle Soup Mix
with Vegetables

Deli Coleslaw   Kosher Pickles

Grilled Turkey 'n Muenster Sandwiches*

Chocolate Chunk Cookies

Sparkling Water with Lime

LIGHT & SIMPLE SUPPER

Lipton Hearty Chicken Noodle Soup Mix
with Diced White Chicken Meat

Assorted Crackers or Bread

Cantaloupe Stuffed with Fruit 'n Cheese*

Raspberry Sherbet

Herbal Tea

AFTER WORKOUT MENU

Lipton Hearty Noodle Soup Mix
with Vegetables in Real Chicken Broth

Mixed Green Salad
with Red Wine Vinaigrette Dressing

Oversized Cheese 'n Dill Muffins*

Assorted Fresh Fruit

Milk

CASUAL PIZZA DINNER

Lipton Hearty Minestrone Soup Mix

Pizza Loaf Provençal*

Olives   Celery & Carrot Sticks

Mocha Ice Cream

Iced Tea

*Recipe appears on page 93.   Cantaloupe Stuffed with Fruit 'n Cheese

❖ OVERSIZED CHEESE 'N DILL MUFFINS

3½ cups all-purpose flour
3 tablespoons sugar
2 tablespoons baking powder
2 teaspoons dill weed
1 teaspoon salt
1 cup shredded Cheddar cheese (about 4 ounces)
1¾ cups milk
2 eggs, slightly beaten
4 tablespoons melted butter or margarine, cooled to room temperature

Preheat oven to 400°.

In large bowl, combine flour, sugar, baking powder, dill, salt and cheese; set aside.

In medium bowl, blend milk, eggs and butter. All at once, add to dry ingredients; stir just until moistened. Spoon batter into well greased muffin pans (batter should fill muffin cups to top). Bake 40 minutes or until muffins are golden.   *Makes 12 large muffins*

❖ GRILLED TURKEY 'N MUENSTER SANDWICHES

4 tablespoons whole berry cranberry sauce
8 slices Italian or French bread (about 1 inch thick)
4 slices smoked or unsmoked cooked turkey breast (about 8 ounces)
4 slices Muenster cheese (about 4 ounces)
6 tablespoons butter or margarine, softened

Evenly spread cranberry sauce on each bread slice. Equally top 4 bread slices with turkey and cheese; top with remaining bread, cranberry sauce side down. Evenly spread 4 tablespoons butter on outside bread slices.

In large skillet, melt remaining butter. Cook sandwiches, covered, over medium heat, turning once and pressing down sandwiches occasionally, 15 minutes or until cheese is melted and sandwiches are golden brown.   *Makes 4 sandwiches*

❖ CANTALOUPE STUFFED WITH FRUIT 'N CHEESE

1 cantaloupe (about 1½ pounds), halved and seeded*
1 cup (8 ounces) part-skim ricotta or low-fat cottage cheese
1 cup sliced strawberries*
   Lettuce leaves
2 tablespoons bran cereal or sunflower seeds

With melon baller or spoon, scoop out 2 cups melon balls from cantaloupe; reserve shells.

In small bowl, combine ricotta, melon balls and strawberries. Fill reserved shells with ricotta mixture and serve on lettuce-lined plates. Sprinkle with cereal.   *Makes 2 servings*

*Substitution: Use 3 cups cut-up assorted fresh or canned fruit and serve in bowls.

❖ CHUNKY CHICKEN SALAD WITH ALMONDS & GRAPES

¾ cup mayonnaise
1 teaspoon dill weed
1 teaspoon Dijon-style prepared mustard
⅛ teaspoon pepper
2 cups cut-up cooked chicken
1 cup seedless green grapes, halved
½ cup slivered almonds, toasted
½ cup chopped green onions

In large bowl, thoroughly blend mayonnaise, dill, mustard and pepper. Stir in remaining ingredients; chill. Serve, if desired, on lettuce-lined plates.
          Makes about 4 servings

❖ PIZZA LOAF PROVENCAL

1 loaf Italian or French bread (about 16 inches long), halved lengthwise
2 cups shredded mozzarella cheese (about 6 ounces)
1 small tomato, coarsely chopped
1 jar (6½ ounces) artichoke hearts in oil, drained (reserve oil)
¼ cup fresh or canned sliced mushrooms
¼ cup grated Parmesan cheese

Preheat oven to 375°.

On baking sheet, arrange bread, cut side up; evenly top bread with mozzarella cheese, tomato, artichokes and mushrooms. Sprinkle with Parmesan cheese, then drizzle with reserved oil. Bake 15 minutes or until cheese is melted. To serve, cut each loaf in half.
          Makes 4 servings

Oversized Cheese 'n Dill Muffins

INDEX